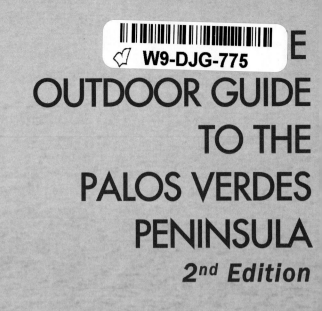

E
OUTDOOR GUIDE
TO THE
PALOS VERDES
PENINSULA

2nd Edition

ii

Outdoor Guide to the Palos Verdes Peninsula
Sunbelt Publications, Inc
Copyright © 2006 by Brad and Kristine Denton
All rights reserved.
First edition 2006. Second edition 2007.

Cover design by Terri Moll tmoll@mn.rr.com
Book design and photography by Brad and Kristine Denton
Printed in the United States of America

Sunbelt Publications, Inc. assumes no responsibility for
hikers' safety on the routes described within.
Corrections and updates to trails and maps are
welcome. No part of this book may be reproduced in
any form without permission from the publisher. Please
direct comments, updates, and inquiries to:

Sunbelt Publications, Inc.
P.O. Box 191126
San Diego, CA 92159-1126
(619) 258-4911, fax: (619) 258-4916
www.sunbeltbooks.com

10 09 08 07   5 4 3 2 1

Cataloging/Publication Data:
Denton, Brad and Kristine
 Outdoor Guide to the Palos Verdes Peninsula by Brad and Kristine
Denton
 -- 1st ed.
 ISBN 13: 978-0-932653-86-4

1. Hiking trails--California--Los Angeles--Guidebooks. 2. Los
Angeles (Calif.)--Guidebooks.
        I. Denton, Brad II. Title.

Cover photographs by Brad and Kristine Denton.
Check our website for local tide and updated route info for hikers:
http://home.earthlink.net/~pvpoutdoorguide/

To Madison & Zoe,

Who are so patient
as Mom and Dad work
and
who are always eager
to go and explore.

Thanks for hiking,
and hiking,
and hiking
with us.

View from Hawthorne Blvd.

Table of Contents

View of Point Fermin Lighthouse from Meyler Street Park

Introduction

We are happy to bring you the 2nd Edition of this trail guide. There have been many changes with trails in the area throughout the last year, and we have received such wonderful feedback and information from the community, we felt it was necessary to update. We also relished the opportunity to improve the book in many ways. So, we have inserted all new pictures, updated the trail information and interior maps throughout the book, and then added new trails and a new chapter. We hope the improvements better serve you in exploring the beautiful area unique to the Palos Verdes Peninsula.

If you are new to the area, we hope that this guide will enhance your appreciation of the wide variety of terrain, people and activities to enjoy on the Peninsula. If you have lived in this lovely community for years, we hope that it may surprise you with a new trail or new location where you can enjoy the view and open space of your unique home.

Thank you so much to the many local residents who encouraged us in making the changes for the 2nd Edition. Your support and knowledge is greatly appreciated. This book has truly turned into a community project and hopefully represents that community well.

Chadwick Canyon Trail

Trail Etiquette

Equestrians, bird watchers, joggers, dog walkers, mountain bikers, small children and others all share the same paths and trails. Their needs and interests are often in conflict, so simple rules have been established to ensure that everyone can use these areas safely. Knowledge of these rules and common courtesy will help prevent the types of accidents that can occur when a horse and rider, bikers, and parents with small children all meet on a trail.

Please be aware that riders on horseback can be encountered on almost any trail. Horses can be skittish or spook with serious consequences for the rider and those around them. **For this reason equestrians are always given the right of way over everyone else**. Per the Horsemen's Trail Guide, when meeting a horse on a narrow trail, stop, move to one side and let the riders pass. Speak to the rider in a friendly and normal tone of voice, so the horse is aware of your presence. Never make loud noises or quick movements near a horse. Never touch a horse without permission or walk closely behind them. When passing a horse from the rear stay at least 25' behind the horse until you talk to the rider and are cleared to pass. Equestrians passing hikers should do the same, giving those in the lead time to get off the trail.

Bicyclists must yield to both equestrians and hikers. Make sure to maintain a safe speed and have control when traveling around blind corners. Also, please be aware that bikes are not allowed on the bridle trails in Rolling Hills or Rolling Hills Estates.

Encounters between horses and dogs, bikers and dogs or even dogs and other dogs can be tricky. Please make sure that dogs are on a leash (it's the law after all) and under control. It is best to give others a wide berth and to calmly and quietly give your dog any commands needed.

The following rules apply to all:
- Stay on the trail or path. Do not create erosion by cutting switchbacks. Trampling off of the trails not only makes much of the land on either side of the trail unusable to wildlife, it is in some cases illegal.
- Do not leave any litter behind. This includes picking up and carrying out dog waste.
- Open flames are not permitted on trails. This includes smoking. Sparks and cigarettes can and have started devastating fires.
- Respect Private Property at all times
- The city of Rolling Hills is private and no trespassing is allowed.

Dangers

There are many different problems you can run into while hiking. The best advice is to always be as prepared as possible. With that in mind, we have put together a chapter of possible dangers that you may encounter along the trail and the recommendations for how to handle the problem should it arise.

Rattlesnakes can be found anywhere and at any time. As the signs state, "Give them distance and respect." 85% of all bites are to males ages 14 – 40, harassing the snakes usually with a stick. The best way to not get bit is to never put your hands or feet anywhere you cannot see them such as in a hole or behind a log. When crossing over a log or large rock step on top of the obstacle and then well away from it. If someone has been bitten, keep them calm, call 911, and transport them to a hospital as soon as possible. Putting ice on the bite will also help.

Poison Oak usually grows near canyon bottoms, as a small nondescript shrub, sometimes as a solid mass of shrubbery. The saying "Leaves of three, let them be" is helpful due to their clusters of 3 leaves, 1/3 to 3 inches long on each stem. The center leaf will be longer than the other two. In the fall, its leaves turn colors, and in winter many leaves may fall off. If encountered, wash everything: shoes, clothes, backpack, dogs, etc. with a strong soap. If a rash develops, calamine lotion or aloe vera will help.

Ticks have the potential to transmit Lyme disease. Not all ticks have this disease and if they do, transmission of the disease to humans usually requires attachment for a day or longer. Prevention is best accomplished by staying on paths and being alert. Usually ticks are found crawling on clothes or felt crawling on skin before they bite in. If they do bite in, quality of removal is more important than speed. Do not use fingers. Use sharp pointed tweezers or a tick removal tool to grasp the mouth as close to the skin as possible and gently pull up. Make sure to clean the bite and tweezers with alcohol. Pets are quite vulnerable to ticks, so check them well. For more information call 1-800-886-lyme, go online at www.lyme.org or contact your vet.

Most of the **cliffs** on the Peninsula are composed of unstable soil and rock. Many serious accidents, and even death, have occurred from people moving too close to the edge of a cliff or trying to climb too steep of a trail. Loose soil can give way in both of these situations, causing one to fall. As a rule of thumb, stay a large step away from the edge of any cliff and never hike a trail so steep that use of hands is necessary.

Fire Ants can be found in many places on the Hill. Look closely at the surrounding area before sitting down, especially if you have children. Fire Ant bites sting, and their venom is dangerous to those who are allergic. For more information, check out www.cdfa.ca.gov .

West Nile Virus has been found in Los Angeles County. The disease is transmitted by receiving a bite from an infected mosquito. It is recommended to take the following steps:
1) avoid parks between dusk and dawn when mosquitoes are most active
2) wear mosquito repellent
3) wear a long sleeved shirt and pants
4) avoid areas with standing water

For further information contact Los Angeles County West Vector Control Disease at 310-915-7370.

Trail Differentiation & Map Key

In this book the trails have been separated into two groups: Large Area Trails and Neighborhood Trails. Large Area Trails are those that are located within a generally broader, open area and are easily accessible to the public. They have parking available at the trail head, some have signage and even trail maps on site, and many are used for guided tours by local organizations such as the Sierra Club, the Los Serenos de Pointe Vicente and the Palos Verdes Peninsula Land Conservancy. Local Nature Preserves, such as Portuguese Bend, Forrestal, George F Canyon, White Point and Lunada Canyon are also included in this category. These Large Area Trails usually have a number of smaller, side trails and it may take many visits to explore all aspects of a locale.

The Neighborhood Trails are mostly located within local communities near homes, are generally not as easily accessible, and are used primarily by local residents. Usually these trails are singular and do not have multiple routes or branches.

No matter what you're looking for in a trail, one can be found here to meet it. Both trail groups contain routes varying in length, views, environment and scenery. All terrain types, from coastal to sidewalk, are included in this book as well. Those who are looking for a main, easily located hike, a long distance trek, or a small trail in walking distance from their home, will find it here.

Trails contain a map and trail description. By checking the maps provided, you can confirm which trails and areas connect to each other and create combinations that suit your specific needs.

A new chapter has been added specifically on loop trails. It lists just a couple of our favorites, usually combining more than one hiking area. There are many, many others available on the Peninsula, especially if you are willing to do a little sidewalk and street walking.

On each map page there will be bullet points listing the following information about the featured trail:

- Approximate Distance of Trail
- Difficulty of Trail
- Notes about the Trail

MAP KEY

_____ **Road, Street or Freeway**

============= **Dirt Road, Road Closed to traffic**

---------------- **Trail, Route, Footpath**

___ _ ___ _ ___ _ **Boundary of City, County or Park**

<<<<<<<<<<<<< **Canyon**

PARK **Parking**

START **Start of Trail**

ALT START **Alternate Starting Point of Trail**

View of Eagle's Nest in Portuguese Bend Nature Preserve

Chapter 1

Large Area Trails

The Large Area Trails are listed roughly by size, starting with the largest area to explore on the Peninsula, the Portuguese Bend Nature Preserve. There are many trails in these large areas and many different hikes can be enjoyed by using different routes. We show and describe the most common main trails, just to get you started. Take some time to explore these larger areas and discover new combinations and connections each time you hike.

Please do be careful to stay on established trails. Creating new trails by bushwacking or cutting corners is harmful to the environment and decreases the amount of space available to the native wildlife.

Trail 1

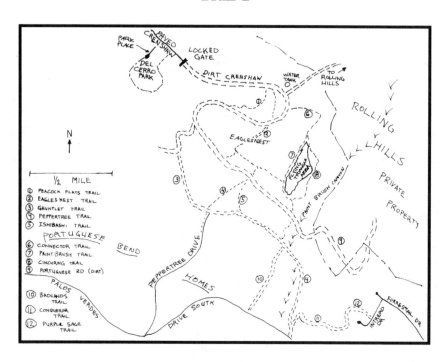

- **Distance:** Main trail – 2 1/2 miles one way; Side trails – 20 miles possible
- **Difficulty:** Easy, moderate and difficult options; Dirt roads, hiking trails and footpaths; All routes start atop the hill: must return uphill
- **Notes:** Nature Preserve; most extensive open hiking area on the Peninsula; wide variety of area types; beautiful views of the Peninsula, Ocean and Catalina; porta-potty at 1st bend in main trail; Mostly sunny

PORTUGUESE BEND
NATURE PRESERVE

This trail starts at the gate which ends the paved portion of Crenshaw Blvd. Here, about 1200' above sea level, Crenshaw Dirt Road begins, and within two minutes of walking you are able to see a large part of this expansive area.

A good destination, for first time visitors, is the prominent hill Eagle's Nest, crowned with pine trees and seen just below the first large U turn. More energetic types may wish to continue over this point and hike down the footpaths on the far side or return to the main dirt road and continue further down the hill. Heading down to Palos Verdes Drive South and back is about a 5 mile round trip.

A unique destination is the area of the most visible landslide movement, about a mile and a half away. Some of the trails in this area are steep and have a slippery surface with loose rock and dirt, so this area is rated difficult. Start from the top take the trail leading down and out to the left from the beginning of the first U turn. This trail is past the water tower but well before Eagle's Nest. As the trail dips, rises, and divides over ridges and canyons, stay to the main footpath/road highest on the hill. It will lead to an area called Flying Triangle, named for both the exposed triangular land formation here and the branding iron that was once used by the early ranchers in this area. Continuing east from here is not possible due to the impassable canyon and cliffs beyond. However, traveling down towards Palos Verdes Drive South is possible, although still steep enough to be rated difficult.

This entire Nature Preserve has scores of ridges, canyons, trails and special places waiting to be explored. Many trips are needed to see them all and even then they change throughout the Seasons and years.

The entire area looks very different after the winter rains, with all the new growth, than it does in the late summer when everything is dried out. For those who wish to explore even further, the Forrestal Property can be reached from the lower left corner of this property; the beach can be reached by exiting through the chain link fence in the same area.

Please be aware that most the property to the west of Portuguese Bend, below Del Cerro Park, is private property. This includes Rattlesnake, Tori's, Kelvin Canyon, Jack's Hat and Annie's Trails. There are signs posted at the perimeter of the property. Please be respectful and stay off of private property.

View of Portuguese Bend and Forrestal Preserves

Trail 2

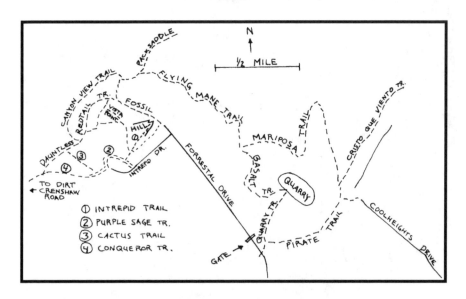

- Distance: Forrestal Drive - 3/8 mile, Many miles on trails possible
- Difficulty: Easy paved and dirt roads, moderate to difficult hiking trails
- Notes: Nature Preserve; Trail map with points of interest available at trailhead; Expanded mountain bike trails; Trail improvements taking place; Sunny

FORRESTAL NATURE PRESERVE TRAILS

Forrestal Nature Preserve is unique in that its main entrance trail is paved and normally closed to traffic, except during the soccer league games and other occasional events held at the large fields connected to the adjoining Ladera Linda Park. The paved road, left over from a housing tract that nearly occupied this space, provides an opportunity for those in wheelchairs or who have limited mobility to explore this area, and due to its gentle slope, it is also a great place to teach a child to ride a bike.

There are two main ways to explore this wonderful area. The first and easiest route is to start down the paved road, behind the normally locked yellow gate, on Forrestal Drive. The second way is to head up the dirt hiking trail to the right of the yellow gate, north of Forrestal Drive.

The first route connects Forrestal Drive to another paved road, Intrepid Drive, which turns left and heads down to a cul de sac with a nice view. For those wishing to continue, use the dirt road, Purple Sage Trail, branching off of Intrepid just before the end. It becomes Conqueror Trail and leads further out of this area to meet the lower ends of dirt roads originating from the Crenshaw Trailhead.

A different hiking option is to continue straight off the end of Forrestal Drive. The trails to the left offer many loop options. One trail heads up to the top of the lone hill and down the other side either connecting with Dauntless and then Conqueror Trail or circling back toward Forrestal Drive. Canyon View Trail is another choice and it again leads toward connection with Dauntless and then Conqueror Trail or can connect with Cactus Trail to circle back. The trail heading right goes uphill to connect with Packsaddle, Flying Mane and the Mariposa Trails, all high above the cliffs next to Forrestal Drive.

The second route starts before the yellow gate. There are well drawn trail maps usually available here, that include a suggested loop path with a self-guided nature trail. The trail passes through an opening in a guard rail and soon forks. The path to the right is Pirate Trail, which leads up into ever expanding vistas until it reaches a sign declaring the city limits of Rolling Hills, which is private property.

The trail to the left, Quarry Trail, parallels Forrestal Drive and leads to the upper slopes of this area and the Quarry Bowl which is a good destination for a short hike or bird watching. Those wishing to continue from the quarry, can follow the path zigzagging in the same general direction that Forrestal Drive heads, northwest. At the end of this trail, the options are uphill and scenic to the right, or downhill meeting up with the end of Forrestal Drive.

This nature preserve is home to endangered coastal sage scrub habitat, home to a number of threatened species including the Cactus Wren, California Gnatcatcher, and the Palos Verdes Blue Butterfly, all of which can be seen here. Local groups are actively working in this area improving the quality of its habitat by removing nonnative and invasive plants and replacing them with native and endangered ones. Willows have been planted along the course of the mostly underground stream here to recreate its original Willow Riparian habitat. This process creates more shade, shelter, homes, and food for more wildlife.

Frascati Trail

Trail 3

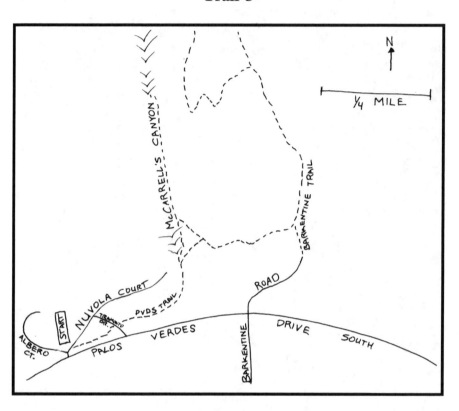

- Distance: ½ mile one way
- Difficulty: Moderate slopes
- Notes: Ocean views; Parking restrictions on
                 some roads in this area; Part of the
                 Portuguese Bend Nature Preserve;
                 Sunny

THREE SISTERS RESERVE TRAILS

Exploring from the end of Barkentine Road, go straight following the dirt footpath rising from the dead end and heading up the hill. Once you are further into the canyon and past the homes, the area really opens up. The vista becomes ever more expansive as the footpath climbs up the canyon in this 98 acre property. It is basically an all upslope climb. You can only hike about half way up to the ridge before being turned around by Private Property signs. Do not trespass and stop here to enjoy the view, before heading back down the hill.

Another entrance is to follow the nicely improved trail running along the inland side of Palos Verdes Drive South. The trail's wood railing can be seen from the road. It starts near Albero Court, passes by Tramonto Drive, and turns inland before an electrical substation. The trail turns uphill into the deep canyon and becomes much more difficult. It becomes a rocky utility access road and follows the high overhead power lines. Branching off to the right of this utility road, by the first couple of poles, are trails which merge and lead into the Barkentine Canyon area.

Trail 4

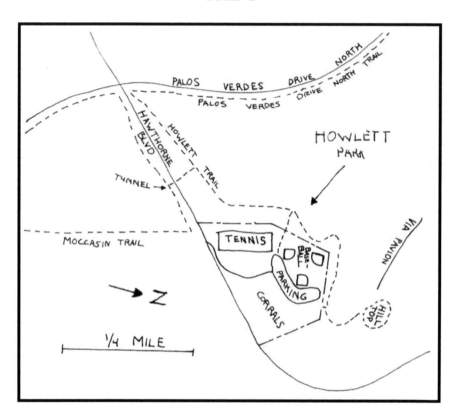

- Distance: Short stroll to all day hiking
- Difficulty: Mostly easy
- Notes: Access to equestrian bridle trails; Mostly sunny trails with some shade

ERNIE HOWLETT PARK TRAILS

Ernie Howlett Park is surrounded by bridle trails. The many options arising from here are all fairly easy. First time visitors may wish to walk to the top of the nearby hill just to the north. This is done by turning right into the parking lot and driving as far as possible before parking. Walk onto the crushed gravel trail just beyond the parking lot and go right through the opening in the white fence. From here, simply take every uphill branch of the trail starting next to the chain link fence. Soon you will be on top of the hill overlooking the Torrance Airport.

Another option is to walk down the dirt road just beyond the same parking area, making all possible lefts. This trail goes along the outside of the park and returns you on the far side past the baseball diamond.

Rolling Hills General Store as a destination makes a good three mile round trip hike, with a nice rural feel to it. Start through the white fences in the back left corner of the parking lot, between the baseball field and tennis courts. This short stretch of trail quickly comes to a T. Go left at the T and follow the bridle path past a couple of turns to the tunnel under Hawthorne Blvd.

Give right of way to any horses near the tunnel. Go through the tunnel and turn left down the Moccasin Trail, which parallels the Hawthorne Blvd. before turning sharply away. The trail passes by the old landfill (now a green field), the rear entrance to Chandler Park, and the Rolling Hills Equestrian Center before passing through another tunnel under Crenshaw Blvd. Continue past the South Bay Botanical Gardens to Rolling Hills Road. Go right up the hill to the General Store. Return to the start the same way or by following the Palos Verdes Drive North trail back to Hawthorne Blvd. then turn right back to Howlett Park.

Many other combinations are available in this area. By looking at the large map you will notice how close Chandler Preserve is to George F Canyon (about a 2 ½ mile hike one way). A shuttle trip with two cars can be a good option.

Trump National Golf Course

Trail 5

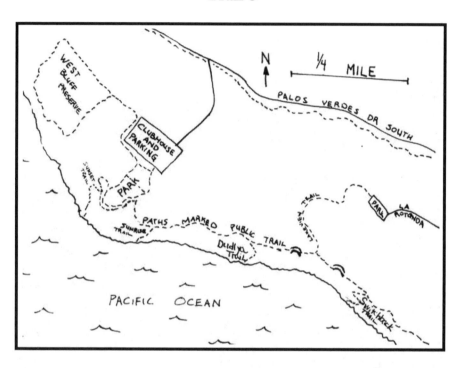

- Distance: Short stroll or many miles of hiking possible
- Difficulty: Easy paved paths, improved hiking trails and moderate footpaths to beach
- Notes: Ecological Reserve; Beach Access; Golf Course; Wheelchair accessible; Bikes on bike paths only; Sunny; Good rainy day option

TRUMP NATIONAL GOLF COURSE: CLUBHOUSE TRAILHEAD

This beautiful area, much of which has been wonderfully restored to its native habitat, is providing home, food and shelter to many birds and animals. The endangered California Gnatcatcher and the threatened California Cactus Wren can both be seen here. Golfers too will be spotted here as the paths wind through and circle the Trump National Golf Course. Please treat golfers as you would all native habitat residents: keep a respectful distance, make no loud noises and watch from a safe location.

After parking in the public parking area on the left of the main clubhouse, different options are available, but first try the path straight towards the Ocean. This paved trail leads down to Founders Park and signs indicate which trails are public and which are for golfers. Paved paths circle and cross this grassy park that has picnic tables, a gazebo and a plaque dedicated to founding Japanese families of the area. Following the paved path on the left side of the park, you reach the top of the bluff.

The trail heading to the right, just below the park, is a short improved dirt trail named Sunset Trail. It leads first to the western most of the four trails that heads down to the beach. It then turns inland to reconnect with the paved trail at the other side of the park. Here the paved path can be followed to the clubhouse or along side it to a west side parking lot.

This trail can be continued to the seven acre West Bluff Preserve, by crossing the footbridge near the far back corner of the west parking lot. (The parking lot here can also be used as a starting point.) The trail is a loop around 7 acres of restored habitat with the West Bluff Trail being a U and Catalina View Trail completing the circle.

The paved trail heading to the left from the Founders Park runs along the bluff top and continues parallel to the Ocean. There are two more dirt trails along this way that wind down to the mostly sandy beach below.

The paved bluff top trail continues on to connect with the La Rotonda trail which leads to that parking lot, and also additional trails along the bluff top which eventually connect with Shoreline Park. All are described in the La Rotonda segment next.

Most of these trails make good options for hiking on rainy days due to their maintained surfaces. You will probably have the paths to yourselves and hiking will not create erosion of the land or muddy wreckage of your shoes.

Trump National Golf Course

Trail 6

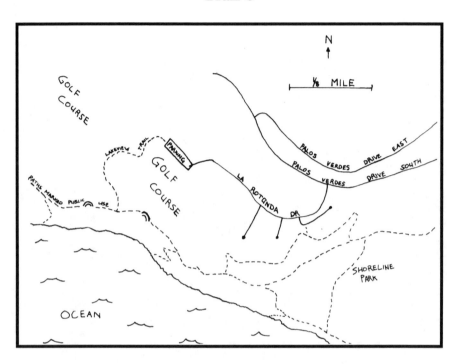

- Distance: Short stroll down the paved path
                   or miles possible on paved paths,
                   dirt hiking trails or shoreline
- Difficulty: Easy paved and improved paths;
                   Moderate to slightly difficult
                   hiking trails
- Notes: Ecological Reserve; Sunny;
                   Ocean views; beach access;
                   wheelchair accessible; restrooms;
                   drinking fountain

TRUMP NATIONAL GOLF COURSE: LA ROTONDA TRAILHEAD

Located at the east end of the Trump National Golf Course, this area provides access to miles of trails. The trail begins at the end of La Rotonda Drive on the Golf Course property. At the start is a nice restroom and drinking fountain provided by the Trump National Golf Course. Please be respectful of golf in play here. Keeping to the paved path marked as the public trail, wind downhill toward the Ocean and at the bluff top you have a choice to turn right or left.

Paths to the east (left) connect with an area that is being returned to it's natural state named Shoreline Park. There are two paths here, upper and lower. The lower one leads to a picnic table and connects to a steep beach access trail before continuing on. The upper trail offers an exit upstairs to Twin Harbors View Road before also connecting to Shoreline Park.

The path to the west (right), travels between the bluff and the Golf Course. It connects with those trails described in the previous section and thus eventually meets Founders Park. Make sure to keep on the paths marked public trail and not those marked golfers only.

Trail 7

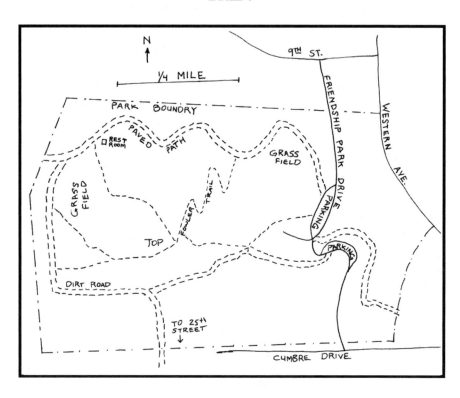

- Distance: Up to 5 miles possible
- Difficulty: Easy main trails to moderate footpaths
- Notes: Harbor and Ocean views; all types of sporting fields; open grassy areas; Sunny; Guided bird watching tours

FRIENDSHIP PARK TRAILS

This 123 acre park is covered in miles of trails. Trail surfaces range from asphalt to gravel to dirt roads and traditional hard packed trails.

There are two public parking lots, the upper one at the Bogdanovich Center and lower one at the Deanne Dana Nature Center. Most people will first want to walk uphill to get a feel for the property and enjoy the scenic views from the top. This can be done from the Bogdanovich parking lot on a foot trail heading straight up the hill to a scenic spot at the top with a bench. The views here are of both the Ocean and the Harbor.

At the top, continuing in the same direction leads to a loop trail which connects to the far end of the property. Walking to the right, away from the ocean, leads to the more developed side of the park with restrooms, a grass lawn and a paved road closed to traffic that leads back down the hill.

Turning left on the loop trail offers an offshoot that turns down and heads back to the parking lot. The left side of the property is less developed and has beautiful Ocean views.

From the Deanne Dana Nature Center parking lot you have two options: using the dirt trail at the Ocean side (left) of the building that traverses up to the hilltop bench or following the paved road at the far end of the parking lot. Staying on the paved road one arrives at the top grass lawn area, near the restrooms.

Trail 8

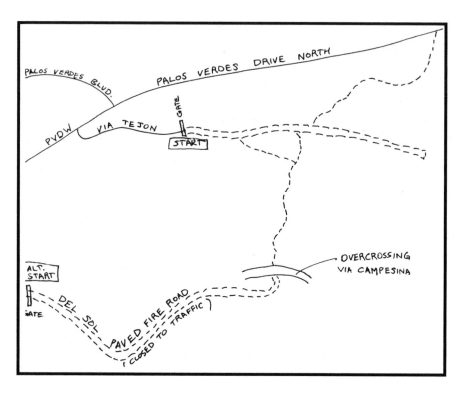

- Distance: 1 ½ miles from Via Tejon to the end of Paseo del Sol fire road
- Difficulty: Easy to moderate dirt roads and hiking trails
- Notes: Mostly shady, opening to sunny fields; year round creek; woodsy feel with a variety of landscapes

MALAGA DUNES TRAILS

This is one of our favorite areas to hike and explore. It is home to many rare wildflowers and is the second location where the Palos Verdes Blue Butterfly has been spotted in recent years. A year round creek shaded by huge Eucalyptus and Pine trees can be found by turning left less than a minute after entering past the gate. A rope swing of dubious safety is usually hanging from a large tree a minute or two upstream.

The main trail goes gently uphill under the shade of giant Eucalyptus trees and across sunny fields, to end at a flat area used by the Palos Verdes Golf Course Maintenance Staff. Under no circumstances walk on to the golf course or distract the golfers.

Several unnamed paths branch off from the main trail. Those to the north (left going uphill) crisscross around and through a large field. The most prominent one comes out near the intersection of Palos Verdes Drive North and Paseo Del Campo.

The two main trails that branch off to the right, both before the top of the hill, lead to the Del Sol paved fire road, which combines for a mile and a half hike one way. They merge into one just before a dry creek bed. Follow this across the plank serving as a bridge and follow the path generally going in the same direction as the overhead power lines. It passes by a very picturesque tree, crosses the dry creek again, climbs a steep hill and goes under the bridge which is Via Campesina. This trail makes a switchback and comes out to the paved and gated fire street named Del Sol Fire Road. If you continue up the paved fire road the ocean views make this a wonderful hike on all levels. The closed fire road ends with a gate at the top, near La Venta Inn.

Trail 9

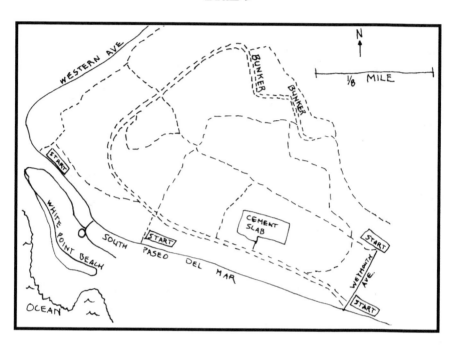

- **Distance:** ¼ mile to top; approx. 3 miles of trails
- **Difficulty:** Easy paved roads, improved hiking trails and footpaths
- **Notes:** Habitat Restoration Area and Nature Preserve; military bunkers on top; sunny open area

WHITE POINT
NATURE PRESERVE TRAILS

Occupying 102 acres, the White Point Nature Preserve is very open and sunny, with views of the Ocean and Catalina. The trails in this area are flat at the front of the property, with hills to the side and back. There is a new handicapped accessible loop around the flat area. It is easy to see where one trail connects with another as the vegetation is low to the ground and there are few trees. The trails, accessed by walking through the open breaks in the fence, crisscross and encircle the property. A loop on the trails can be done heading in either direction. There is a paved road now used for a trail that runs parallel to the Ocean near the entrances before cutting up the hill across the west side of the property to the two massive bunkers. The paths behind and on top of the bunkers provide the best scenic vistas and also the best up close viewing of the vintage fortifications on top. There are plaques, as you walk along the trails, with information about the habitat, animal life and history of the area.

The Palos Verdes Peninsula Land Conservancy (PVPLC) continues to work on this property improving trails and the area's natural state of perennial grassland with wildflower and Coastal sage scrub habitat. The many little flags in the ground mark where planting has been done, sometimes accompanied by a simple watering device that looks like a milk carton. Please take care to stay on the trails, even though it is flat and easy to step off.

Trail 10

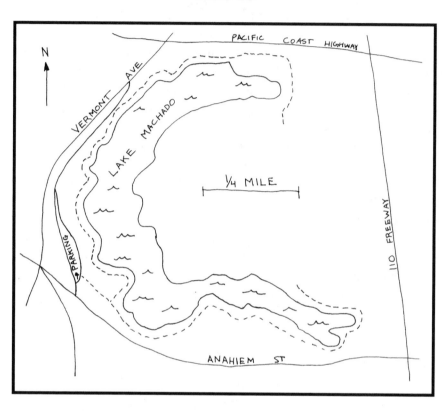

- Distance: Main path is 1 ½ miles
- Difficulty: Easy, mostly paved trails
- Notes: Lake; Bird watching site, tours
                available; Children's playground
                equipment in park

KEN MALLOY HARBOR
REGIONAL PARK TRAILS

The harbor park area and what is now Lake Machado was the center of Native American activity in this region. It was the site of their largest local village long before the Spanish discovered California.

One of the main reasons for this area's popularity, then and now, is the wildlife one finds here. Over 300 different species of birds live in or visit this area during migration, making this is a prime location for naturalists, birdwatchers and families just out for a stroll along the lake.

Three sides of the lake offer flat, paved paths. They start near the edges of the parking lot and meander in and out from the shore. These are easy, flat paths to walk on and it is fine to head off the paths onto the grass, making this an easy place to bring children. There is even a children's area featuring playground equipment located near the middle of the property.

A multi-year project has been approved for this property to improve water quality and habitat area in and around the lake. Hopefully, we can expect an even better park for watching wildlife in the future.

Trail 11

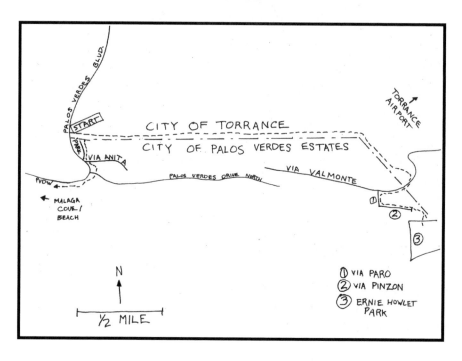

- Distance: 2.5 miles one way
- Difficulty: Easy, dirt utility road
- Notes: Airport and some Ocean views;
  multiple starting and turnaround
  points possible; Lots of trees –
  mostly shady

ROLLING HILLS ESTATES / TORRANCE UTILITY ROAD

This is the longest straight line path on the Peninsula. Multiple starting points are possible along this long utility road that makes a very nice hike. The lower end starts on Palos Verdes Blvd and Via Anita. The surface switches back and forth from dirt to mulch or bark. Backyards line both sides of the trail providing beautiful shrubbery and trees along this mostly shady road.

Heading east, after about a mile and a half on the trail, the Torrance Airport will be seen below and the dirt road will turn into a footpath. This path soon forks with the right trail ending further up where it meets the street, and the left fork continuing to Via Valmonte. This is the location of the El Mirlo tower gatehouse, a national landmark in the shape of a tower, and once a main entrance to Palos Verdes. It is possible to continue on to Howlett Park from here by walking up Via Valmonte to Via Paro. Take Via Paro left to Via Pinzon. Go left again to its end at the prominent hill. From here, turn right down the hill, under the overhead wires, and pass through the white fence into Howlett Park.

This trail can be combined with the Malaga Dunes Trail or beach trails in Malaga Cove. At the trailhead, turn right and walk parallel to Palos Verdes Boulevard across Via Anita. The dirt trail begins here and remains parallel to Palos Verdes Bvld as it bends to the left. The trail turns down to the crosswalk at Palos Verdes Drive North. Once across the street it connects with an improved trail that leads to the sidewalks at Malaga Cove Plaza. Turn left on Via Tejon to connect with the Malaga Dunes Trail or cross Palos Verdes Drive North at Via Almar and head down the sidewalk until a footpath is spotted on the right which heads down to the Ocean.

Trail 12

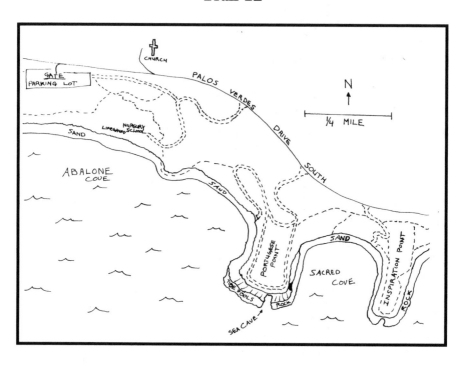

- Distance: ¼ mile to sandy beach – many miles
                 of hiking available
- Difficulty: Mostly easy to moderate hiking over
                 paved and dirt roads, improved hiking
                 trails and footpaths
- Notes: Ecological Reserve; $5.00 parking
                 fee; Porta-potty on top; Sandy beach
                 below with a lifeguard; No dogs, bar-
                 b-ques, or collecting; Sunny

ABALONE COVE TRAIL

Abalone Cove Shoreline Park is an excellent place to park and explore the south side of the Peninsula, as well as the rare sandy beaches below. The trails are easy, and from here you can find tide pools, sea caves, open fields, miles of hiking, and fantastic views from on top of the two cliff points.

The trail down the hill to the beach is easy and beach exploring is possible in both directions from the lifeguard tower. The first point to the east, Portuguese Point, is impassable along the shore due to an impressive sea cave, as is Inspiration Point beyond it. To explore past these two points use the trails and roads that go over the bluffs and back down to the shore.

To explore the upper area, follow the paved path east as it winds but stays parallel to Palos Verdes Drive South. At Portuguese Point, a dirt road goes along the perimeter of the bluff point, encircling a grassy field. Continuing east is Sacred Cove, a smaller, secluded beach tucked between two large points. The furthest one is named Inspiration Point and a trip to its tip explains why this is aptly named.

A map of the area will be given to you at the parking gate with pictures and descriptions of various tide pool creatures on the back. The map also states that this is an ecological reserve, which means no dogs are permitted and no collecting of flowers, rocks, marine life etc.

Trail 13

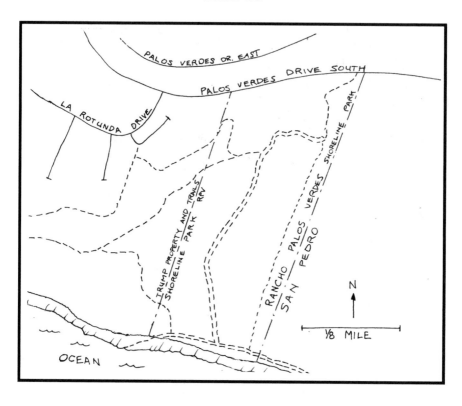

- Distance: ¼ mile to beach; miles of hiking possible
- Difficulty: Moderate to bluff top then steep
- Notes: Beach Access; Parking restricted 6-9AM and 3-7PM; Ocean & Catalina views; Part of Portuguese Bend Nature Preserve; Sunny

SHORELINE PARK TRAILS at RANCHO PALOS VERDES / SAN PEDRO CITY LINE

This trail offers beautiful Ocean views and is wide open and easy to navigate. There are homes all along the left side as one walks toward the Ocean. The trail starts out steep from the street and then becomes flat. The trails to the right can be taken to those on the Trump National Golf Course property (La Rotonda). The upper most trail exits by stairs up to Twin Harbors View Road, which is also another good access point for these trails.

If you continue straight down the main trail towards the Ocean, it becomes steeper again and then flat as you reach the bluff top. If you turn to the right, you will soon encounter a picnic table and the option of turning down to the beach or turning up to the Trump National Golf Course trails

If you turn left at the bluff top, the short path skirts between houses on the left and a cliff on the right. It ends on neighborhood streets near the bluffs before White Point/Royal Palms County Beach.

If you do head down to the beach, coastal exploration is possible in both directions over this mostly rocky stretch of shoreline. To the right are three improved trails leading up to the public paths on Trump National Golf Course. To the left is White Point/Royal Palms County Beach.

If parking on Palos Verdes Drive South be sure to read the parking restrictions on the signs posted along the street.

Trail 14

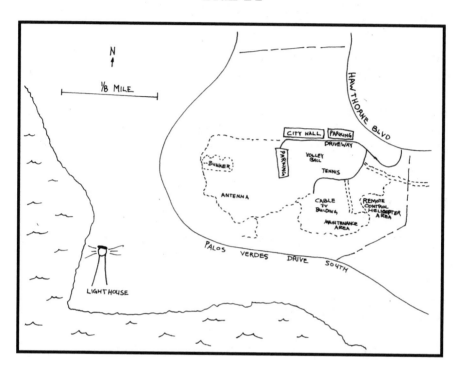

- Distance: Over 1 mile possible
- Difficulty: Mostly easy with some narrow trails
- Notes: Large undeveloped areas and grass fields; Ocean and Lighthouse views; old military bunkers; remote control helicopter area; Slopes are part of Portuguese Bend Nature Preserve; Mostly Sunny

UPPER POINT VICENTE TRAILS

Over a mile of trails cover this mostly undeveloped area. Begin by walking along the paved driveway, towards the Ocean, keeping the largest building (City Hall) on your right. Straight out from the end of the driveway is a narrower paved path that leads to a large concrete military bunker. This site, which extends four stories underground, is locked but its various vents, doors, etc. can be found nearby. Continue walking in a large counterclockwise circle around the upper part of this property. Head past the large wood antenna, and connect to the smaller paved driveway. Walk past the local TV station and other buildings to the large square asphalt pad. This area is used only for the flying of remote control helicopters and most of the operators are very good, doing loops, rolls and flying upside down.

Continue walking past the pad to the edge of the field. On the hillside below and to the right are two-man bunkers, half hidden in the cactus off of very narrow trails. Below to the left can be seen some of the largest remaining cultivated fields on the Peninsula; a reminder of what was once an extensive enterprise. Return to parking by walking up the gravel driveway, near the helicopter area, or explore the large grass field surrounding this route.

Trail 15

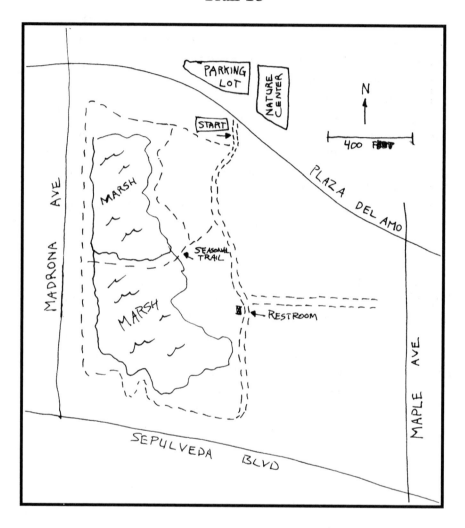

- Distance: Approximately 43 acres of land
                to hike
- Difficulty: Easy, Improved trails and
                footpaths
- Notes: Great bird watching; flat hiking;
                Interpretive Center; Mostly
                sunny with some shady spots

MADRONA MARSH PRESERVE TRAILS

This flat, easy walk in the center of Torrance is another example of how many birds and animals will come to a small native habitat if given an opportunity. The preserve includes 43 acres of seasonal wetlands, vernal pools, dunes and grasslands. The special draws here are the vernal marsh and back dune environments and the birds that live or stop here on their migration.

The trail entrance is across Plaza Del Amo Street from the Nature Center. The trails encircle and cross the back dune habitat, one of the few of its kind left in this area. The trails then continue to the back of the property where the slightly lower elevation creates wetter environments.

Guided Hikes are available to learn the many reasons why this area is so important. They are offered quite frequently, and special walks for kids are also available. Trail Maps and information pamphlets are also available at the Nature Center.

The Nature Center itself has many exhibits, a committee room, activities for children and a demonstration garden of drought tolerant and native plants, not to mention their friendly staff. The Center also offers a full schedule of workshops, talks, bird walks and volunteer opportunities if you are so inclined.

Trail 16

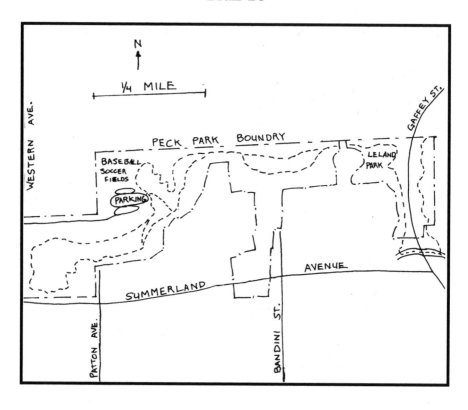

- Distance: 1 mile to Gaffey Street
- Difficulty: Moderate
- Notes: Year round creek; some parts
               overgrown; Park offers various fields,
               courts, playground equipment and a
               public pool; Sunny and shady sections –
               lots of trees

PECK PARK CANYON TRAILS

Peck Park is a woodsy area with large grass fields, sports facilities and a major canyon running down the center of it. This canyon has a year round creek in it and main hiking trails are on both sides of the canyon.

On the parking lot side of the canyon the trails go to the left, down and right. Left is overgrown but interesting as it follows and crosses the creek multiple times. The trail leading down crosses the creek and goes up the other side to the large grass fields. The trail to the right circles around the top of the creek and continues down on the other side.

The trail on the south side of the stream (right side facing downstream) can also be reached from the end of Patton near Summerland. This trail continues down along the park boundaries, past farms with llamas, goats and horses. The well worn path continues until it meets with a chain link fence blocking the canyon at this end of Peck Park. Go right up the short hill to North Herbert Street. Walking a half block to the left brings you to the Leland Recreation Area. This park does continue further into the canyon.

This canyon is a nice setting for a hike but sadly it is sometimes neglected and littered with trash. Feral cats are very common here and homeless people are often seen in the overgrown sections of the canyons. Clean-up campaigns are currently being undertaken.

Trail 17

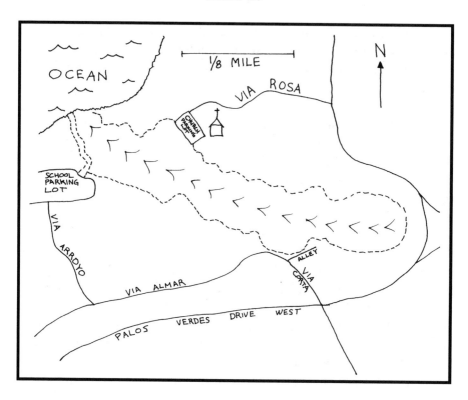

- Distance: 1/8 mile to beach; 1 mile loop
- Difficulty: Difficult – not for children
- Notes: Steep, loose footing; trail passes along
               very edge of tall cliffs; beautiful views;
               year round creek; Sunny

MALAGA COVE TRAIL

This bluff top trailhead can lead you down to the beach or on a beautiful and varied canyon loop hike. The canyon hike can be very difficult as there are both overgrown conditions and steep cliffs in sections. The beach access road is paved and easy and connects with a flat, dirt footpath at beach level. This beach is referred to locally as R.A.T. Beach which stands for Right After Torrance, and does not describe the beach inhabitants.

Starting at the Malaga Cove School parking lot, the paved path to the right of the gazebo heads down to the beach below, while the loop trail begins at the end of the dead end street off of the parking lot. Heading away from the Ocean, keep the canyon on your left and the baseball field on your right. Head through the grassy area, before this trail leads up and out to a sidewalk. Go left on the sidewalk and then left again down the alley. The hiking trail restarts past the chain gate on the left side of the alley. Follow this trail around the end of the canyon as it curves to the other side. (There is an option here to stay on the sidewalk. Instead of heading down the alley to connect with the trail, stay on the street sidewalk and turn left on Palos Verdes Drive West. Follow that sidewalk as it curves left and connects to Via Rosa, the street entrance to the church.)

Now heading back toward the Ocean, walk through the field area, keeping the church and its parking lot on your right. Now the trail becomes more difficult as it narrows. The path skirts past a couple of backyards and through some overgrown areas. The footpath then passes along the edge of a very tall and unstable cliff leading to a nice vista point, before continuing steeply down to meet the sandy beach and the paved ramp leading back to the start.

Along the trail, between the church and the beach, a footpath branches to the left through a prominent notch in a tree and descends steeply past some prickly pear cactus. At the bottom of this path is an interesting spot beside the creek near a few king palms. Be aware of the cliffs in this entire area. They are made of soft dirt and may collapse, raising a danger for those above and below.

Santa Monica Bay

Trail 18

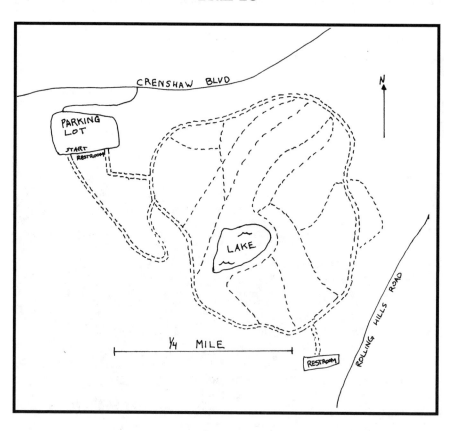

- Distance: 87 Acres /Many miles of paved
                   and improved trails
- Difficulty: Easy
- Notes: Over 4,500 types of plants;
                   different garden areas; Gift Shop;
                   restrooms & drinking fountain: $7
                   Admission Fee; Sunny grassy
                   areas and shady by pond

SOUTH COAST BOTANIC GARDEN TRAILS

This 87 acre property, created on what was once a sanitary landfill, is a great place to hike. There are over 4,500 different types of plants here, ranging from tiny grasses to towering redwoods. In roses alone, there are 1,600 different types showcased. The amount of wildlife that is drawn here is also extensive, as over 200 different types of birds are spotted here annually.

A paved path encircles the property and hard pack dirt and gravel improved paths crisscross through the center. Many of the plants and trees throughout the area have identification signs. The trails lead you through different themed gardens such as rose, herb, fuchsia, vegetable, a wonderful children's garden, and more. The property also includes meadows, a creek and a lake which is home to ducks, koi and turtles.

In addition to the garden's inspiring ideas for home, there are how-to clinics, lectures and concerts offered to the public throughout the year. Plant sales are also offered at the gift shop located at the entrance.

Trail 19

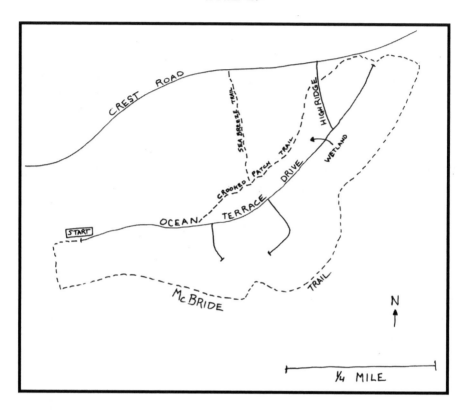

- Distance: Two mile round trip
- Difficulty: Easy improved and hiking trails
- Notes: Sunny; flat; Ocean and Catalina views

MC BRIDE TRAIL

This hike starts from the end of Ocean Terrace Drive. Beginning as a narrow footpath, it soon turns into a wide and level dirt road/firebreak that proceeds along the top of the hills near Crest Road. It passes between beautiful homes on one side and beautiful scenery on the other. The views from this 1000' foot vantage point include the Pacific Ocean, Catalina, Abalone Cove, Annie's Stand, Portuguese Point and more.

Walking the mile long trail, you pass along three prominent ridges known as Three Sisters. (Please see Trail 3 - Three Sisters for legal passage to this area.) As the trail continues, it starts to turn inland. Here the view below is of the Vanderlip Estate and the Portuguese Bend Riding Club.

Near its end, McBride Trail forks. Heading right, the trail soon ends. Heading to the left leads out to Crest Road. After a short distance bear left on a gap between houses. Cross Highridge onto the Crooked Patch Trail, named for the characteristics of the garbanzo beans that the Japanese farmers grew in the area. The trail passes a small wetland with the original tule rushes, before climbing up to meet Ocean Terrace Drive. Return the way you came, or continue walking along the street for a much shorter finish.

Please note that hiking on the dirt paths that head downhill from McBride trail trespasses onto Private Property. Even though there are trails, this does not mean they should be used, so please be respectful. No Trespassing signs are posted.

Trail 20

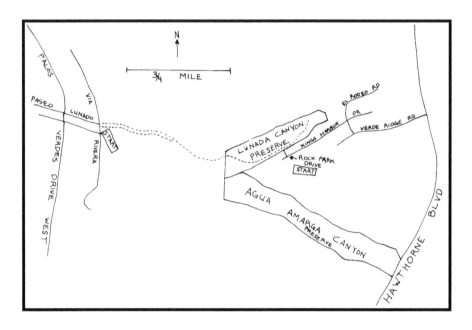

- Distance: ¾ mile from top to bottom of Preserve
- Difficulty: Moderate; steep sections
- Notes: Sunny; Creek; Nature Preserve

LUNADA CANYON PRESERVE AND AGUA AMARGA CANYON

Lunada Canyon Preserve is easily accessed from the end of Rock Park Drive and Posey Way. Entering near the top of this canyon, you can go either up or down through the 20 acres that comprise this preserve. You can also continue further down along Lunada Canyon in Palos Verdes Estates to Lunada Bay. Although Agua Amarga Canyon Property is connected to Lunada Canyon Preserve at the lower end, there are no trails heading up Agua Amarga Canyon. It is best explored through the use of binoculars from Hawthorne or Crest Road.

Another popular starting point to this area is lower down in the canyon at the end of Paseo Lunado, where it meets Via Rivera. This hike follows the foot worn dirt road heading steeply up into the canyon from below. This trail narrows near the top but continues up to the Rock Park Drive entrance and extends for a short distance. The view of the Ocean on the way back down is worth the hike up.

Trail 21

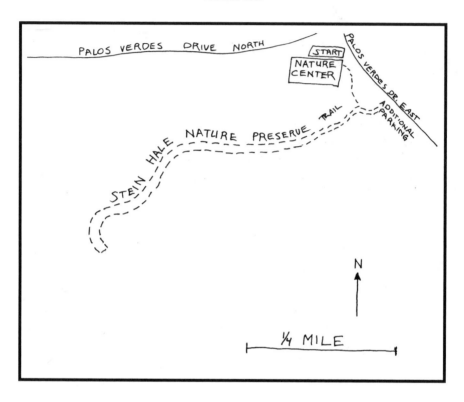

- Distance: ¾ mile to top of trail
- Difficulty: Easy to moderate hiking trail
- Notes: Mostly shady; Nature Preserve; Trail
  map with points of interest; Year
  round creek; View from the top;
  Nature Center at start with
  restrooms; No bikes allowed

GEORGE F CANYON NATURE PRESERVE: STEIN/HALE NATURE TRAIL

This canyon hike begins with a Nature Center full of exhibits and a gift shop. It is a wonderful discovery center for children with live animals, stuffed animals to examine up close, puppets, and many drawers of nature items to study. The center also has information on docent led hikes, night hikes, guided bird walks, and a story time which offers a hike for children.

The hiking trail itself starts from the Nature Center and from the adjacent gravel parking lot on Palos Verdes Drive East. The bulletin board at the start of the trail has trail maps that include information about the numbered stops that are passed during the hike. During the mile and a half round trip, the trail guide will describe and point out poison oak, willow riparian habitat, 150 million year old bedrock, coastal sage scrub habitat and much more. Two stream crossings over the year round creek, common equestrian traffic, lots of wildlife and city views at the top all combine to make this an enjoyable hike.

Trail 22

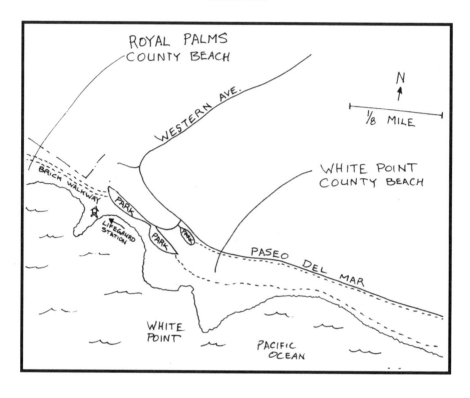

- **Distance:** 1/8 mile brick walkway in lower area, miles of beachcombing and bluff top walking
- **Difficulty:** Easy walkway, rocky shoreline
- **Notes:** Two parking lots: upper is metered, lower is $6.00; children's play area, picnic tables & restrooms; Sunny

WHITE POINT / ROYAL PALMS COUNTY BEACH TRAIL

White Point Beach is directly across the street from the White Point Nature Preserve. The upper parking lot near the fountain is metered, and the street parking is free. On this upper section there is a restroom, children's play area, picnic tables, and benches. The plaques at the vista points overlooking Catalina and the Ocean telling of the unique history of this area are well worth the read. Walking and jogging are popular along the bluffs from here to Pt. Fermin Lighthouse, 1 ½ miles away.

To get to the lower section, you can walk down from the upper area or drive down on Kay Fiorentino Drive. There is a gate at the top and a fee of $6.00 to park below. Dramatic geological formations can be seen at the lower parking area.

To the west (right facing the Ocean), is a coastal area once home to the Royal Palms Hotel. The brick walkway leads past open air fireplaces that once were home to outdoor parties and dances. Further down the walkway, picnic tables are set in a quiet area under the palms. Beyond that the beach returns to its natural state.

To the left, facing the Ocean is a wider beach easier to explore. The offshore rocks here and in the center of the property are sanctuary to numerous coastal birds. The underwater nature trail is in the second bay, left of the lifeguard tower, known locally as Divers Cove. It is currently somewhat overgrown, but many of the plaques are still readable although the rope connecting them is gone.

Trail 23

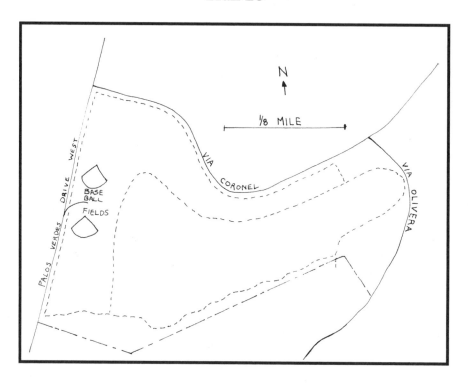

- Distance: Over 1 mile of trails
- Difficulty: Easy to moderate on hill
- Notes: Great place to jog; used by Palos Verdes High School cross country team; Sunny

LUNADA BAY LITTLE LEAGUE
AREA TRAILS

A variety of loop trails can be made in this area. The largest convenient loop is made by following the trail along Palos Verdes Drive West. If walking clockwise, pass by the ball fields and follow the trail on the far side of the canyon, paralleling Via Coronel up the hill. The path turns right at Via Olivera, and travels across the top of the property to the far side. The path now starts heading back downhill and goes from open sun to shady on the side closest to Palos Verdes Intermediate School. The trail continues along the fence separating the two areas.

As you overlook the baseball fields, you can choose either trail heading down hill, as both lead back to the start, a total distance of about 1 mile. Other trails cross through the center of the canyon, which can be used to create additional loops. There is a full par fitness course along the main trail, making this a great place to get some exercise.

Trail 24

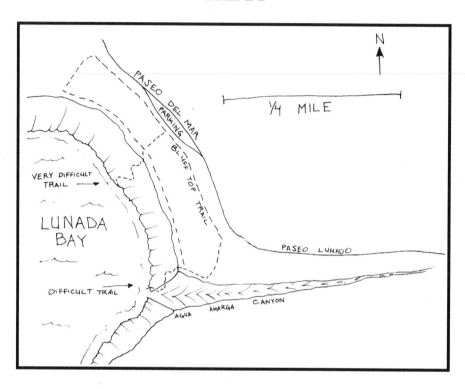

- Distance: 1/8 mile to beach: Miles of hiking possible on top of bluffs and at shoreline
- Difficulty: Bluff top walk easy; Difficult trail to beach
- Notes: Tide pools; Beachcombing; Picturesque canyon; Sunny

LUNADA BAY BEACH TRAIL

Parking is easy along the side of Paseo Del Mar at this location.
Start by walking along the bluff top path, as it provides an easy trail
with views of the beach and waves below. Two trails lead down the
bluffs providing access to the beach. The trail in the center of the
field is most difficult, while the trail in the far left corner is slightly
easier, but is still very steep. Although neither is safe, both are
heavily used.

On the right side of the rocky beach a surf fort can be found. Around
the corner beyond that are the remains of the Dominator. Very little
is now left of this 441 foot freighter that ran aground here at Rocky
Point in 1961.

On the beach, immediately to the left of the trail, is the terminus of
Lunada Canyon. Walking up and into this canyon is amazing. Bring
a camera because this unique and interesting place offers a great
opportunity for quality photography.

The tide pools two miles further left, below Oceanfront Park, are
very large, but the shoreline hike along this stretch is very difficult
by trail standards because it is often necessary to watch your feet
while hopping from rock to rock.

Trail 25

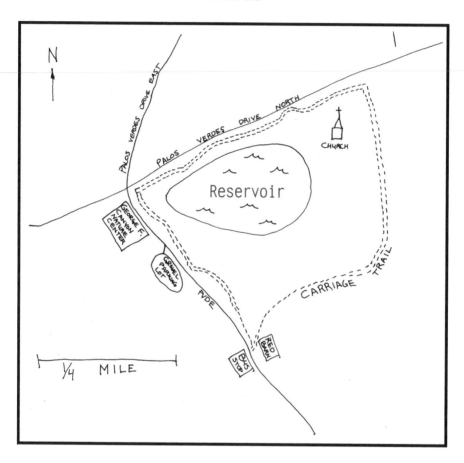

- Distance: 1 3/8 mile
- Difficulty: Moderate, mostly flat but with some
               steep sections
- Notes: Across the street from George F
               Canyon; Reservoir views; Part sun
               and part shade

RESERVOIR LOOP TRAIL

This trail circles around the main Palos Verdes Peninsula Water Reservoir, and is enjoyed by equestrians and hikers alike.

Starting from the George F Canyon Nature Center where parking is available, cross Palos Verdes Drive East at the crosswalk. This loop may be done in either direction. If going clockwise, walk down the wide level bridle path paralleling Palos Verdes Drive North. Pass by Rolling Hills Covenant Church and turn right past the end of the parking lot. The path continues down into a shallow canyon past the mortuary and up the other side. A fence forces another turn to the right heading now back towards Palos Verdes Drive East. This stretch named the Carriage Trail is narrower and steeper and passage now by a carriage would probably be impossible. After passing some barns and stables, the trail comes out to Palos Verdes Drive East. Turn right again following the path which sometimes follows the street and sometimes tucks away into the woods. This path leads back to the corner of Palos Verdes Drive East and Palos Verdes Drive North where it began.

Trail 26

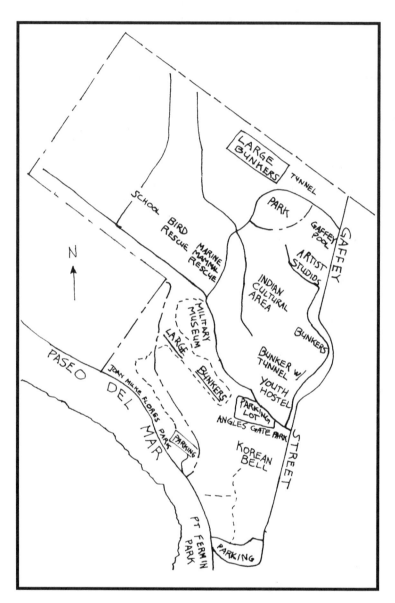

- Distance: Short stroll to extensive exploring
- Difficulty: Easy
- Notes: Large Diverse Area; Sunny;
  Information Center; Military Museum;
  Rescue Centers; Restrooms

FORT MACARTHUR TRAILS

Many starting points, routes and destinations are possible in this very large and diverse area. The three main parking lots are accessed from Gaffey Street. The first one is at the Korean Bell, the second as you continue to follow the road is at the Marine Mammal Rescue Center and International Bird Rescue Center and following the road further is the third parking area below the Marine Vessel Traffic Center. At the Korean Bell area is a large grassy area, a children's play area, basketball courts, an Information Center about the Korean Bell and youth hostel buildings, as well as restrooms. This picturesque area is popular with tourists, kite flyers, and residents bringing relatives from out of town.

Heading past the grassy hilltop areas and the chain link fence, you can head up on the paved streets, by car or foot, and find the second parking area. In addition to the rescue centers, there is a large area to hike around that holds the Military Museum and large batteries. The museum is an excellent place to learn about much of our local history. It has very interesting exhibits and photographs. A gift shop is attached to the museum. From the large grassy area here is a trail and paved road that head down to the Joan Milke Flores Park.

The International Bird Rescue and Research Center is closed to the public but the Marine Mammal Rescue Center is open to walk through quietly. Seeing the many sections full of resting seals and sea lions on their way to recovery is always inspirational. A small gift shop can also be found here and volunteer opportunities abound.

Continuing up the paved road is the Marine Exchange – Vessel Traffic Center. Here there are artists' buildings and an Indian Cultural Area with erected structures and gathering areas outside. Three different parks are found within this property along with large bunkers and tunnels that are rarely crowded.

The attached Joan Milke Flores Park has its own parking area off of Paseo Del Mar and can be used as another entrance to then explore this large area. Heading up from the parking lot is a paved road to follow with grassy areas on each side. It curves up to the top of the hill where it connects with a bunker and Military Museum area.

Trail 27

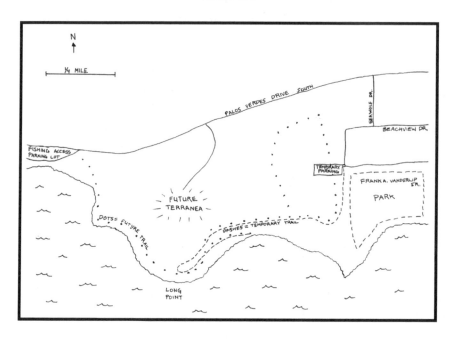

- Distance: Temporary trail currently about 1 mile
- Difficulty: Easy, rocky beach
- Notes: Under construction at this time; Large open cave down at beach; Sunny trail

LONG POINT/TERRANEA RESORT TEMPORARY TRAIL

This area is completely under construction while the building of the Terranea Resort & Spa is underway, however they have kept a temporary beach access trail available to the public during this time.

The temporary parking lot is at the corner of Nantasket Drive and Seacove Drive with 10 parking spots, and an additional handicapped space. The temporary trail, enclosed on both sides by a chain link fence, heads straight off of the parking lot towards the ocean.

Follow the trail zigzaging down to the beach, where you will discover a beautiful cave if you head to the left which is fun for the kids to explore. Do check tide tables (a link can be found on our website) and watch your step. Heading to the right is possible for a short way before being blocked by the cliff.

In the future, the bluff top section should connect with the Frank A.Vanderlip, Sr. Park Trail. The Terranea website states that "Public access programs will be embraced at Terranea Resort promoting awareness of this unique ecology through a Nature Center and on-site naturalist."

67

Trail 28

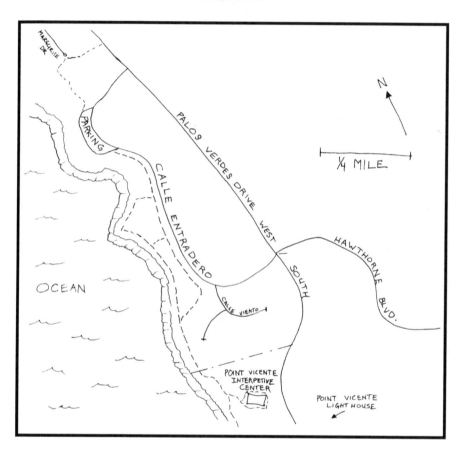

- Distance: Over 1 mile of trails
- Difficulty: Easy, flat improved trails & sidewalks
- Notes: Sunny; Native Habitat area; Ocean views; Porta-potty by parking lot

OCEANFRONT PARK TRAILS

The wide improved trails and sidewalks here are flat and offer an easy hike and wonderful Ocean views. The parking lot is located on the west side of this bluff top trail area. This area is sunny with wood fencing surrounding a reinstated natural habitat area.

From the parking lot, head out left facing the Ocean (east) on the improved trail or the sidewalk which run parallel with each other. This improved trail will cut off to the right, following the cliff line and the trails make a figure eight if viewed from above. The sidewalk connects again with the improved trail at the middle of the eight and at the very end. There is also public parking along the road across from the center of the eight.

These trails also connect to the Point Vicente Interpretive Center trail via a small wood bridge near the south end. This bluff top trail continues past the Interpretive Center to the Coast Guard Property, which is gated off. The Point Vicente Lighthouse, located on the property, is open one Saturday a month.

Trail 29

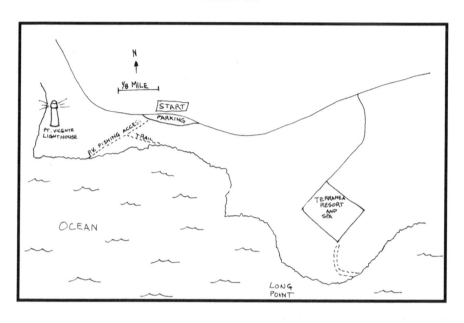

- **Distance:**   1/8 mile roundtrip to beach, further exploration along Coast in both directions
- **Difficulty:**   Moderate
- **Notes:**   Beach access; tide pools to the left; restroom at parking area; Sunny

POINT VICENTE FISHING ACCESS TRAIL

This is one of the few areas to park for free along this stretch of coast. It has a good vantage point to monitor the passage of whales on migration. Fishermen, of course, also use this spot along with many others who simply want to look at the view, snap a few pictures or stretch their legs. On the hill behind the lot, three slabs of concrete can be seen. These are the tops of base end stations for the guns at Point Vicente and Fort MacArthur. They can only be reached from Upper Point Vicente Park.

The trail down to the beach starts from the restroom and drinking fountain area. It traverses down the hill at a gentle slope making one switchback. The trail is wide and level with a railing on the downhill side providing a safe trail down to the beach. The shoreline here is rocky making it necessary to watch your footing while walking the beach.

Beachcombing is possible in both directions. Travel to the right nearly a mile before reaching the point below Point Vicente Lighthouse. Approximately ½ mile to the left, there is Long Point, which is impassable due to a 15 foot high cliff.

Trail 30

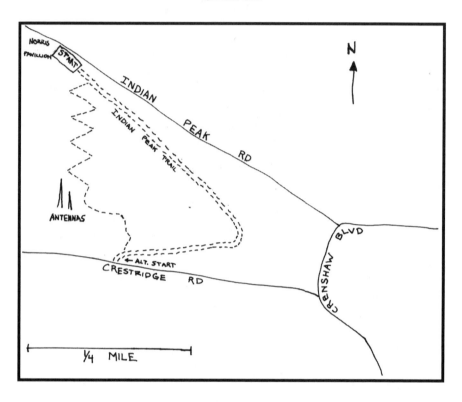

- Distance: Main path is ½ mile
- Difficulty: Moderate
- Notes: Incredible Views from Santa Monica
  Bay to L.A. Harbor; Sunny

INDIAN PEAK TRAIL

Starting next to the Norris Pavilion, across the street from the Norris Theatre, the trail Y's right after the start of the trail. To the left is an overgrown dirt road which traverses up the hill at a steady grade. It turns to the west near the top and meets with Crestridge Road forming a walking path to and from the stores in Deep Valley.

The trail to the right zigzags to the top where the panoramic views are breathtaking. Seasonal trails commonly crisscross through the center of this property as well and head to the top.

After the winter rains spur new growth, the main trails are the only paths, as the less commonly used trails become overgrown. By the end of summer, much of the plant life dries out and seasonal paths reappear due to usage across the hill.

Sections of this property may soon be developed, so please be sure to watch for signs and do not trespass.

Trail 31

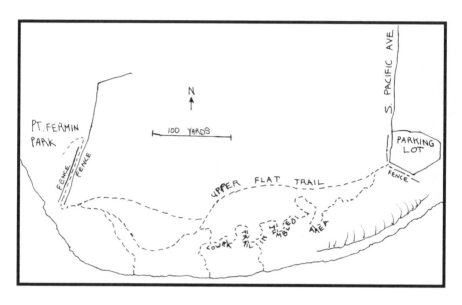

- Distance: 1/8 mile
- Difficulty: Moderate to difficult
- Notes: Explore as part of an organized group with a permitted docent only – do not trespass

SUNKEN CITY TRAIL

A couple of organizations conduct walks through this area that is only a few blocks long, but is still worth seeing because of its unique nature. Foundations of roads, railways, sewers, and homes can be seen here twisted and destroyed by the Point Fermin landslide of 1929 which was reactivated in 1940.

Signs are posted on both sides of this property stating no trespassing, so only explore this area as part of an organized group that has a special permit to enter this area. Many routes are possible through the maze. Access is possible from Sunken City to the rocky beach, which is a marine life refuge. If you are unable to visit this area as part of a group, some of it can be seen from the fence by the lot at the end of Pacific Avenue.

Trail 32

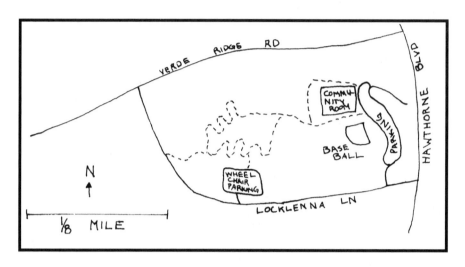

- Distance: 1 mile of trail
- Difficulty: Easy
- Notes: Sports fields; Community Center;
               Bar-b-que areas; Wheelchair
               accessible; Sunny

FRED HESSE JR. PARK TRAILS

Facing the community center from the parking lot, there are large grassy fields to the left with wonderful Ocean views. The trails in this upper half of this park, around the community center and the grassy fields, are all paved. They encircle the area, but also connect and lead to more than one children's play area and bar-b-ques behind the community center.

The paved trail on the far right of the community center runs along the property line heading toward the Ocean. This trail leads to the lower half of the property. The sunny trails here are covered in crushed gravel and are wheelchair negotiable. They travel in switchback turns going over small foot bridges that span the tiny dry creek. Bronze plaques of famous literary quotes are set into stone along the path. A loop is easily done back up to the paved trails by the community center. There is also a volleyball area located here for picnics.

The community center has meeting rooms used by many local organizations and the Rancho Palos Verdes City Council and the Home Owners Council hold their meetings here.

Via Tejon Fire Station Trail

Chapter 2

Neighborhood Trails

The trails in this section are located within neighborhoods, have limited street parking, and are used primarily by local residents. These trails are in alphabetical order.

As many of these trails are surrounded by backyards and homes, please be respectful of the residents by keeping on the trails and off of private property. Never cut through a yard or across someone's property.

Many local residents use these trails for dog walking. Please make sure that your dogs are under control at all times and always on a leash. Keeping your dogs away from the backyard fences that line many of these trails also helps to not excite dogs in their own backyards.

Trail 33

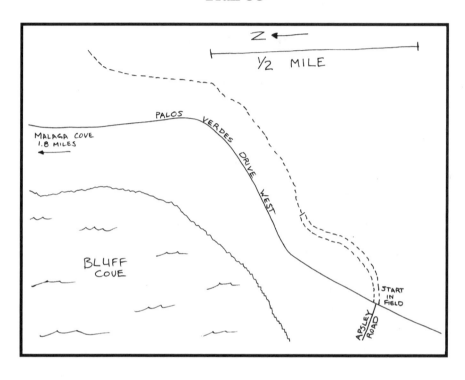

- Distance: 1 mile dirt road, 3/4 mile
- Difficulty: Moderate uphill
- Notes: Great bluff cove view; tick area; Sunny

APSLEY ROAD DIRT EXTENSION

This hike starts at the small open lot on the inland side of Palos Verdes Drive West and Apsley Road. The trail starts by skirting past two back yards on the left side of the field. It continues up an overgrown dirt road to a wonderful vantage point with a large flat area. A great foot path goes further from there through some interesting areas beneath wind sculpted pine trees and traversing across the hill covered by many different types of shrubs and grasses. The trail ends by slowly dwindling away.

Unfortunately, in our experience, this trail also has more ticks than anywhere else on the hill. Every year or so I return here hoping they have left and every time I return with five to ten unwanted creatures crawling around on me.

Back at the start, traveling up the hill to the right is also possible. Most of the trails leading up into this area are thin and overgrown.

Trail 34

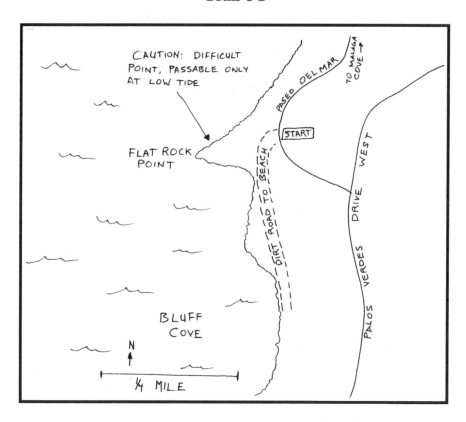

- Distance: 1/8 mile to beach, further beach hiking possible in both directions
- Difficulty: Moderate to beach, rocky on beach
- Notes: Dirt road; popular local surf spot; Sunny

BLUFF COVE TRAIL

Bluff Cove is a popular spot for local surfers. This long, wide, dirt road branches off of Paseo Del Mar a mile past Malaga Cove. Here, on the Ocean side, is a gate blocking vehicles from traveling down the dirt road which serves as a trail to the shore.

The cove area is wide and sandy beach areas can be found. Rocky shoreline hiking is possible in both directions and there are some tide pools to explore.

If going to the right be aware of the tide, as this point is dangerous or impossible to pass at high tide. Going to the left is safe in regards to tides. It can be hiked all the way to the remains of the Dominator on Rocky Point, and beyond to Lunada Bay if you are determined. Please consult a tide table, found on our website at home.earthlink.net/~pvpoutdoorguide and weather guides and use good common sense as coastal hiking can be dangerous.

(The large rock in the right corner of this picture, taken at low tide, is not passable at high tides.)

Trail 35

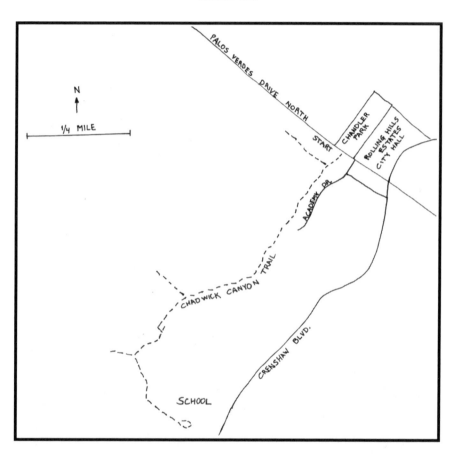

- Distance: 1 mile trail
- Difficulty: Moderate
- Notes: Mostly sunny trail; Ends behind
                Chadwick school

CHADWICK CANYON TRAIL

Starting as a bridle trail, this route begins on Palos Verdes Drive North about 100 yards west of Crenshaw Blvd. At the first prominent Y in the trail, go to the left to continue to the footpath. (To the right is the continuation of a short bridle path which dead ends.)

This sunny, flat trail follows a year round creek which disappears and reappears depending on water conditions. Another small footpath heads off to the right after another bend, but again stay to the left. The trail then cuts up a short, skinny, steep hill and at the top is another Y. Head to the right, as the left dead ends after a few yards. The trail borders on a shear bank dropping off into the creek here, but the trail is wide and level. During late summer a handful of blackberries are easily picked and make a delicious snack along the way. (Do not pick any berries unless you are certain of their identification – some, such as the very commonly seen castor bean, are extremely poinsonous.)

After this sunny stretch, the trail bends to the east and up the canyon. Here it crosses the creek bed over and back again. The trail then continues, passing barns and corrals no longer in use. There are more trees farther along the path and nice spots of shade. The trail dead ends at the school property grounds of Chadwick school. There is a kiosk here that shows a map of the canyon area and describes some of the students' activities in the canyon.

Trail 36

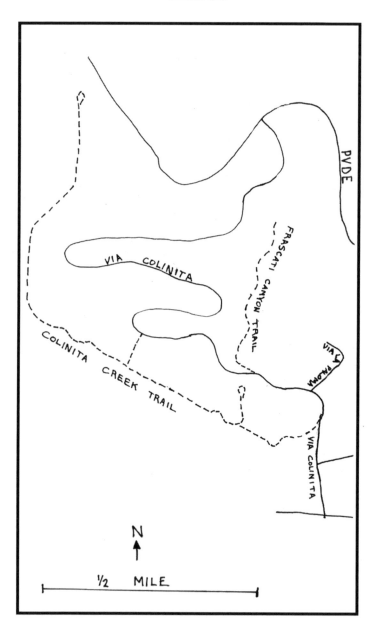

- Distance: 1/2 mile
- Difficulty: Easy to Moderate Uphill
- Notes: Surrounded by yards in sections;
                Mostly shady

COLINITA CREEK TRAIL

This newly graded utility access road is a joy to hike. Start on Via Colinita near Miraleste Drive. Walk between the boulders and steel posts set to frame the entrance to the constant grade path heading downhill. Passing through the park like area at the canyon bottom, the trail Y's. Continue up the steep hill, following the overhead power lines. The trail to the right may soon be completed to connect with the Frascati Canyon Trail across Via Colinita. As the trail dips down and turns, enjoy the expansive Harbor views on your left.

Yards and houses become further set back as the trail continues and you head uphill again. The trail currently ends at a private driveway, but may continue further up to Palos Verdes Drive East in the future. For now turn around and head back out on the same trail. This trail is great for hiking with kids as it is shady, easy to walk on and not too long. Plus spotting ships and the Angeles Gate Lighthouse along the way make it quite fun.

This trail can be combined with the Sienna Canyon trail by walking straight across Via Colinita. The entrance has matching boulders and posts and is directly across the street from the start. Other options are to walk across Miraleste and connect with the Miraleste Median Trail or with the Lorraine Road Trail.

Trail 37

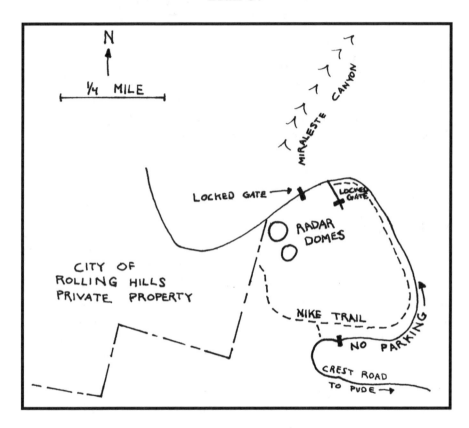

- Distance: ¼ mile
- Difficulty: Moderate
- Notes: Short trail; usually overgrown; Sunny

CREST ROAD TO RADAR SPHERES

A narrow footpath climbs steeply up the hill from Crest Road just before the No Parking signs start. It originates from the last parking spot. The trail angles up and left, meeting with an old dirt road continuing in the general direction of the radar spheres. The spheres themselves, are of course fenced off, however the view at this location is from nearly the highest vantage point on the hill.

Back down at the start, an improved trail begins from the roadside around the uphill corner. It is a short trail, roughly following Crest Road, for about 1/4 mile. Using this trail and the road's shoulder brings the hiker to the gate which effectively ends Crest Road.

Trail 38

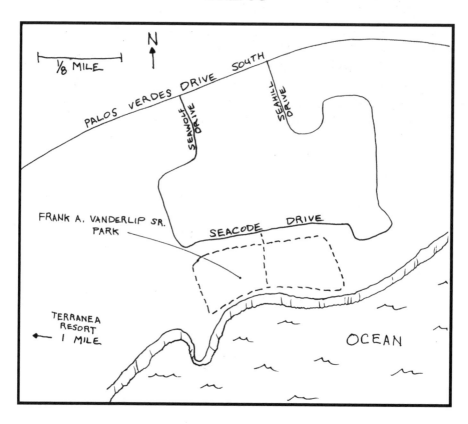

- Distance: 1/4 mile round trip
- Difficulty: Easy
- Notes: Very small park; nice bluff top walk; Sunny

FRANK A. VANDERLIP, SR. PARK TRAIL

This tiny park, not shown on most street maps, is the trailhead for a pleasant and short bluff top walk. Rarely used and nicely maintained, it commands a nice view. Walking to the right leads past beautiful homes inland and shoreline views of the beach far below. The wide and level hard pack dirt trail continues right for about one block before turning inland. It follows along the side of one property and connects with the sidewalk which returns back to the start.

Walking left along the bluff top does much the same, however, it is possible to go slightly further in this direction. After completing this quarter mile hike back to the start, you can take advantage of the convenient bench that is located in a nicely situated area overlooking the Coast.

Trail 39

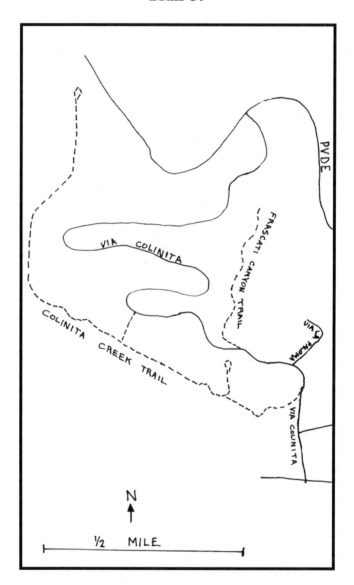

- Distance: Approx. 1/2 mile
- Difficulty: Easy
- Notes: Short at this time; Shady; Year round creek

FRASCATI CANYON TRAIL

This secluded canyon trail is mostly shady and follows a year round creek, making this a good choice during hot summer months. This trail is still under construction as of this writing, but the portion which is done, like all trails built by the Miraleste Parks and Recreation Department, is of excellent quality in both design and workmanship.

The start is a little tricky to find as the trail immediately drops out of view from the road. To find the trailhead, go up Via Colinita from Miraleste Drive, pass the first curve to the left and watch for the opening on the right after the next bend.

The first 50 feet going downhill are the steepest, and then the trail starts following a gentle uphill grade along the creek. Although not completed as of this writing, plans show it to be a loop trail continuing up towards Via Colinita and Palos Verdes Drive East. It may also in the future connect across the road from its start to the Colinita Creek Trail. This would then connect it to the other five wonderful trails in this Miraleste area.

Trail 40

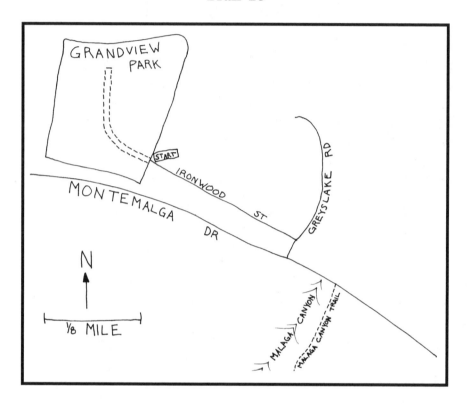

- Distance: Less than 1/4 mile
- Difficulty: Easy
- Notes: One single trail to the top with a nice view; undeveloped park

GRANDVIEW PARK TRAIL

This small to medium sized, undeveloped park is basically a large grass field with a single, dirt road to its top. A nice view of the South Bay beaches far below and the Palos Verdes Golf Course can be seen by the dog walkers and joggers that primarily use this property.

The main trail is the dirt road which continues from the dead end of Ironwood Street to the top of the hill. Small, short trails branch off from here achieving a slightly different angle on the view below.

Being an undeveloped park, there are no amenities here. For a longer hike in this same area, the Malaga Canyon trail on the other side of Montemalaga Drive continues about ¾ of a mile up and into the canyon coming out at Mossbank Drive.

Trail 41

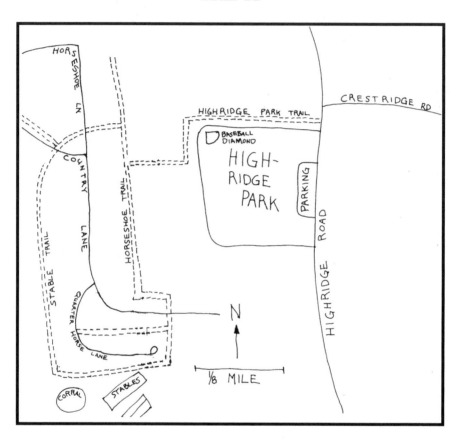

- **Distance:**   ¼ mile inside park; longer distances outside of park
- **Difficulty:**   Easy
- **Notes:**   Nice traditional park; Access to bridle trails; Wheelchair accessible; Restrooms; Sunny

HIGHRIDGE PARK TRAIL

This developed park is popular with local residents. Large mature trees and hard packed sand trails, accessible to wheel chairs, are all nicely integrated into this pretty park.

The main trail is down past the children's play area. It is a small ¼ mile loop trail that offers stopping points with par course fitness work-outs. For further walking, you can follow the bridle trails that border the park. They are located behind the baseball diamond at the back of the park and are all rated easy in the surrounding area.

Trail 42

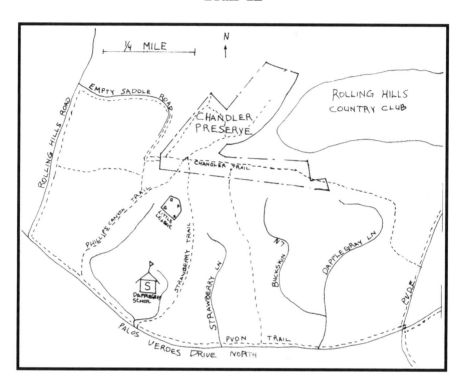

- Distance: Approximately 1 mile within
                  Preserve
- Difficulty: Easy to Moderate
- Notes: Mainly equestrian traffic; Sunny

LINDEN H. CHANDLER PRESERVE TRAIL

Donated by the Chandler family, this 28 acre piece of land is set in a rural area where horses, and commonly peacocks, will be found. An information kiosk with a very good map of the area can be found below the baseball diamond.

Trails skirt by the Rolling Hill Country Club, Dapplegray Elementary School, and the backyards of homes lining the bridle paths here. Most of these trails continue out of this area's boundaries and lead to Howlett Park, George F Canyon and the General Store.

Access may be gained by walking downhill along the trails on either side of Dapplegray School or by using the trail continuing beyond the end of Empty Saddle Road. Once in the Preserve, the Golf Course Overlook Trail forms the northern boundary and the school and ball fields make the southern. The Chandler Trail leads due east and turns into Dapplegray Trail leading uphill to Palos Verdes Drive East and George F Canyon Nature Center. Heading west from Chandler leads to Rolling Hills Road and the General Store.

Trail 43

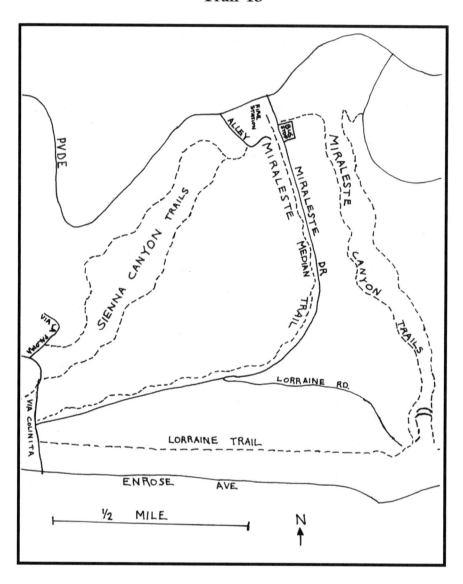

- Distance: 1/2 mile
- Difficulty: Easy, flat, wide utility road
- Notes: Popular with local dog walkers;
               backyards on both sides; Shady

LORRAINE ROAD TRAIL

Mature trees line this straight and mostly flat utility road. The wide trail is made up of bark dust, dirt and mulch. It is a popular place for local residents walking their dogs or jogging. It is a quiet walk with some views of the Harbor. There are houses on both sides of the trail, so please be respectful of private property.

Start at the green gate on Via Colinita near Miraleste Drive. The trail proceeds flat and level for nearly ½ mile before a dip and rise. Here the Access Road ends, but continuation is possible as it connects straight into the Miraleste Canyon Trail.

A loop back to the start can be made by going up the Miraleste Canyon Trail to Miraleste Plaza and then down the Sienna Canyon Trail or by connecting to the Miraleste Median Trail. Both options end at Via Colinita. Crossing Miraleste Drive at Via Colinita brings you back to the starting point.

Trail 44

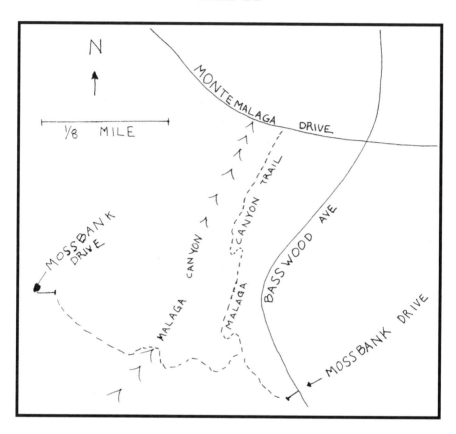

- Distance: 1/2 mile
- Difficulty: Moderate
- Notes: Scenic quiet canyon; Sunny

MALAGA CANYON TRAILS

Malaga Canyon Trail, starts on Montemalaga Drive, across the street from the Pacific Unitarian Church. The trail traverses up the left side of the canyon with a couple of minor switchbacks. As you near the top of the hill, the trail comes to a Y and the most commonly used fork continues on to the dead end of Mossbank Drive off of Basswood Avenue. The other fork leads to a dead end of Mossbank Drive also, this time off of Grayslake Road.

In the spring, this canyon is full of flowers and the buzzing, just from the bees, is very loud. Walking up the stone strewn center of the canyon is also possible.

Trail 45

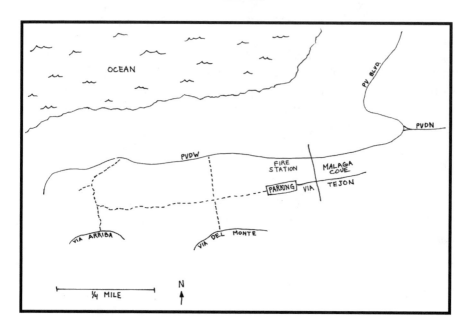

- Distance: 1/2 mile trail
- Difficulty: Easy to Moderate
- Notes: Mostly shady; Stair connections to neighboring streets

VIA TEJON FIRE STATION TRAIL

Convenient parking and an unmistakable start are two of the reasons this is a popular trail. This mostly shady trail also offers a wide walking surface and great views.

Parking is available at the end of Via Tejon, behind the fire station, and the trail begins right off of the parking lot. Half way up the trail are stairs that connect to the local streets, Palos Verdes Drive West below and Via Del Monte above. The main path continues on to a Y. To the left are another set of stairs up to Via Arriba, while the right path u-turns with the trail winding downhill. The trail continues gradually down until it comes to an end at Palos Verdes Drive West. Turning around here to do a roundtrip is probably best as walking along PVDW is not recommended and can be quite dangerous.

The trail is mainly used by local residents for dog walking and/or a great connection off streets for jogging.

Trail 46

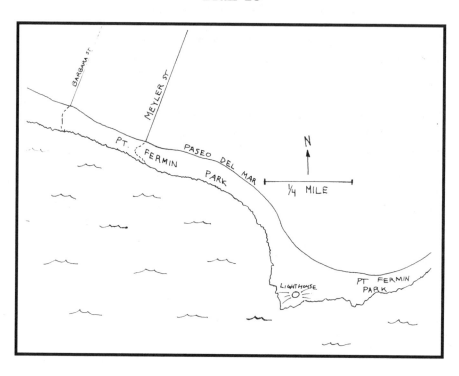

- Distance: 1/16 mile to beach
- Difficulty: Easy
- Notes: Beach access; our smallest butterfly, the Pygmy Blue, is sometimes found here; Shady park area on bluff

MEYLER & BARBARA STREETS
BEACH ACCESS TRAILS

These two San Pedro beach access trails are only five blocks from each other. They both begin on the bluff top in a nice park setting. Meyler Street is located halfway between Point Fermin Lighthouse and White Point County Beach, each a ½ mile away.

The beach access trails are both partly paved and easy to walk. Unfortunately, broken glass shards are commonly seen on these paths making them a poor choice for dog walking. The Meyler Street entrance has a restroom and less glass than Barbara Street. It is also closer to Point Fermin which can be reached by walking left along the shoreline. The tip of the point is reachable only at low tide and calm conditions. Fisherman and others have been swept off this point and drowned, so use good judgment.

The beach along this stretch of Coast is mostly rocky. The Pygmy Blue Butterfly makes its home here on the slopes between the bluff top and shore.

Trail 47

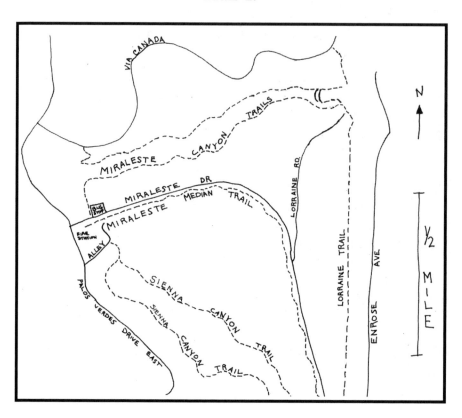

- Distance: ½ mile
- Difficulty: Easy
- Notes: Shady, wide, quality hiking trails

MIRALESTE CANYON TRAILS

Two trails, very well designed and constructed, run up and down this section of Miraleste Canyon. The trails run on either side of the seasonal creek in the center.

This hike can be started with easy access from Miraleste Plaza behind the bus stop. Follow the trail into the beautiful, shady canyon heading east. At the lower end of the trail is a bridge which crosses the creekbed to the trail on the other side. At this juncture, there is also access to either the street Via Canada (cross the bridge and head up to the right), the Lorraine Road Trail (continue straight on the trail), and Trudie Street (head straight and turn off toward the left) if you are not continuing on this trail.

For those continuing on the Miraleste Canyon Trail, cross the bridge and head west (left), up the other side of the canyon. At the end, the trail will head uphill and zigzag to end on Via Canada. Turn left and walk a short distance to connect with Palos Verdes Drive East. Turn left and follow the sidewalk. You can look down here at the canyon just hiked as well as enjoy beautiful views of the Harbor. At Miraleste Drive take another left to finish the loop back to the bus stop.

Many combinations of hikes can be made by connecting either side of this trail with neighboring trails such as Lorraine Road Trail, Sienna Canyon and Miraleste Drive Median Trail.

Trail 48

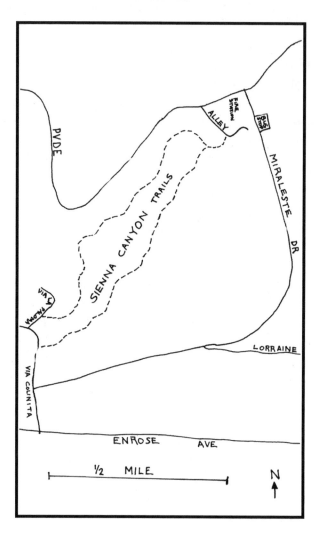

- Distance: ¾ mile canyon loop
- Difficulty: Easy, some up and down
- Notes: Loop or can be combined with neighboring trails for further distances; Mostly sunny with some shade

SIENNA CANYON TRAILS

This wide, dirt access road loops the canyon and is used quite regularly by local residents. It can be accessed at three different locations, and can be used as a connector to other trails in the area or as its own loop.

Starting from the alley behind the automotive repair shop in Miraleste Plaza, the trail drops swiftly into the canyon. You can see the trail on the other side of the canyon for most of the hike. To make this a loop trail, there is a short stretch of street walking on Via Colinita and Via La Palma at the lower end, which provides the other two access points.

The trail can be connected to the Lorraine Road Trail or with the Miraleste Median Trail by turning left when you come out on Via Colinita and crossing Miraleste Drive.

Trail 49

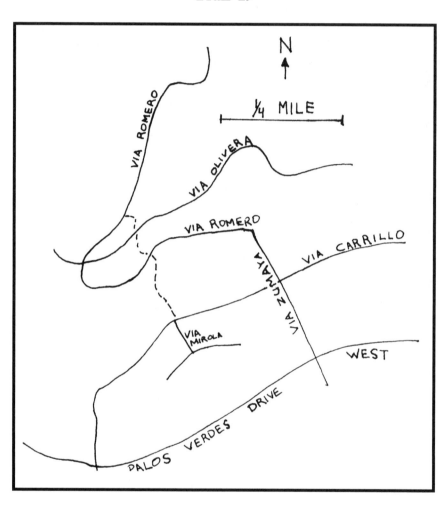

- Distance: ¼ mile
- Difficulty: Moderate Uphill
- Notes: Great Ocean view; sidewalk path; Mostly sunny

VIA ROMERO TRAIL

The lower end of this paved trail begins from a small, nicely maintained park at the intersection of Via Carrillo and Via Mirola. The wood stairs at the rear of the park zig zag to the top of the hill. Cross Via Cabrillo and pick up the trail on the other side of the street. As you continue uphill following the trail, it crosses Via Romero twice in the same manner. The trail ends as it meets Via Romero for the last time.

The trail provides quite an uphill workout and the views of the Ocean from the top are wonderful. Mainly used by local residents, this trail provides a nice walking route, although take care when crossing the roads, as cars are coming around blind corners.

Agua Amarga Canyon

Chapter 3

Extended Hikes

The hikes in this chapter are longer than those previously described and will usually require more than one day to complete. We have broken them into smaller sections which can be completed individually. The hiking terrain will vary greatly from hike to hike. Even within a hike itself, you can go from a flat, wide sidewalk to a barely there, dirt footpath. However, if you are one of those people that loves working towards a goal – then this is the chapter to guide you along.

Extended Hikes

Trail 50

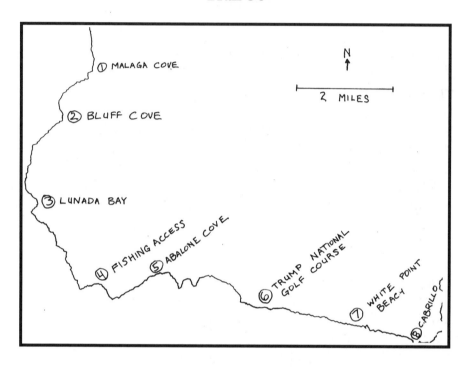

- Distance: Longest Segment is 3 miles; Total of all segments is 17 miles
- Difficulty: Most difficult in the book
- Notes: Entire Coast is broken into seven manageable sections

COASTAL ROUTE

Hiking the entire shoreline is most easily done in segments. We have divided this hike into seven segments each about two or three miles long. This makes it possible to spread the hiking out over days, weeks or years, thus making the trip more manageable. A word of caution here: these are the most difficult and dangerous trips in the book. Many people have died or injured themselves on our Coast from falling off cliffs, being swept off rocks by the Ocean, or by being out during the wrong tide or weather. If you're not in good, strong physical condition, do not try this route. Most of it involves hopping from rock to rock, many of them loose and tilting. There are very few sandy stretches where you can hold your head up and look around, as you are usually watching where to set your feet.

Tides are very important on this trip. Do not attempt it without a tide table, available at home.earthlink.net/~pvpoutdoorguide, and a watch. Most of the points, even the minor ones, can only be passed at low tide. Start each segment an hour or more before low tide to allow yourself time to finish before the tide starts rising again. Also, hike only on days the Ocean is calm and surf is low.

Before starting a segment, drive to the exit point and pick out a landmark that you will recognize from the shoreline. This is helpful as many of the trails going up the bluffs from the Ocean look very similar. Look also at alternate exit points. These might be important if you twist an ankle or the surf picks up. It's easiest to park a car at each end of the segment for a shuttle, but if you are walking back to your car, follow the street. The rising tide will have probably made a shoreline return impossible and walking along the street will be easier and faster.

Distances shown are for one way only, double the mileage if walking back. As a last note, realize that conditions change. If something seems too dangerous, it is. Stop. Go back and wait for another day or walk around it on the bluffs above.

Segment 1: Malaga Cove to Bluff Cove (approx. 1.5 miles)
Park at the lot behind the Malaga Cove School and follow the paved path down to the beach. Turn left, and after passing the Palos Verdes Beach & Athletic Club swimming pool, the first point is flat point rock. Like most points on this trip, it is only passable at low tide. The last point on this segment can also only be passed at low tide. The exit is the noticeable dirt road traversing from the shore up to Paseo Del Mar.

Segment 2: Bluff Cove to Lunada Bay (approx. 3 miles)
After parking, follow the long dirt road that heads in the correct direction. This is a longer segment than the first, but the tides are not as much of a factor while going around these points. Numerous bootleg trails will be passed that lead to the top. These, like all the others, should not be used. Many are not safe and their use causes a considerable amount of erosion.

At Rocky Point you will see the small amount of rusted wreckage left from the 441' Dominator, the largest ship to crash into the Peninsula. Further on, you will find a stone surf fort. At Lunada Bay, exit by using the trail on the far side of the bay, as it is slightly easier than the center trail.

Segment 3: Lunada Bay to Point Vicente Fishing Access (approx. 3 miles)
Use the trail down to the beach on the left side of the bluff top. Resort point, the first headland, is easy to pass. In the next cove over are large boulders from a fairly recent rockslide. Next, just below Oceanfront Park, are some of the largest and best tide pools to be found. The exposed tip of Point Vicente can only be passed at low tide and calm conditions. A sudden increase in the amount of trash on the beach indicates the proximity of the improved trail up to the exit at the Point Vicente Fishing Access lot.

Segment 4: Point Vicente Fishing Access to Abalone Cove Shoreline Park (approx. 1 1/4 miles)

This sounds like a short section, but the approximate distance doesn't count the backtracking that must be done on this leg which almost

doubles the distance. At Long Point is a 15' tall cliff which at spring low tides may be passable, but usually it is not. Touch the cliff, walk back to your car and drive to the lower parking lot at Long Point. Walk as far as possible to the right this time, touch the cliff and walk as far as possible the other way. Most people will be stopped just past the large sea cave. Touch the cliff and drive to Abalone Cove/Shoreline Park where you will once again start out to the right. Once you touch the cliff this segment is done. Don't worry about not walking the few feet that were missed at the tips of the points. All the backtracking qualifies you as having actually made the entire distance.

Segment 5: Abalone Cove to Trump National Golf Course (approx. 3 miles)

This segment involves some minor backtracking, much less than the last segment. Upon reaching the first headland, Portuguese Point, you will notice the 15' channel full of surging waves, sharp rocks and spiny urchins. Walk to the tip of each of the points with their sea caves and tide pools before walking up and over the points using the bluff top trails. A detour to the tip of Inspiration Point bluff top is worth the effort. The rest of this leg is fairly easy. Pass down the trail, after the last point, Inspiration, through the corner of the property used by the South Bay Archery Club down to the partly sandy beach. Head past the Portuguese Bend Club to Trump National Golf Course. The first of the three improved trails, which leads into the Trump Property, is the most direct route up to the western most parking area.

Segment 6: Trump National Golf Course to White Point County Beach/Royal Palms (approx. 2 miles)

Park in the public lot and start down the trail you took up on the last segment. Three trails lead down from this property, and another from Shoreline Park. This stretch is mostly rocky and no backtracking is necessary. Along the way are a few houses that are surprisingly close to the water. As you get near the end, walk along the brick walkway that was Royal Palms family club for a relaxing finish to this segment.

Segment 7: White Point County Beach/Royal Palms to Cabrillo Beach (approx. 3 miles)

This is a fairly easy stretch. Start where the last segment ended at White Point Beach. Walk past the limestone walkway which leads down from Barbara Street. Point Fermin can only be passed during the lowest of spring tides and completely flat surf. Touch the tip at the farthest point you can safely reach, and then walk back to the metal stairs which lead up to Meyler Street. Walk along the bluff top trail, pass through Point Fermin Park and use the trail at the far end of the park heading down. Walk right along the beach as far as you can, touch the cliff, and then continue your trip in the original direction. Pass below Sunken City and continue to the end of the fishing pier at Cabrillo Beach. Here you can congratulate yourself for having made the trip.

Portuguese Point

Trail 51

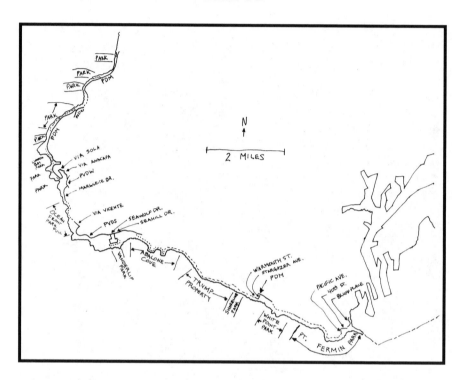

- Distance: 16 miles
- Difficulty: Improved trails, sidewalks and dirt footpaths; Easy to Moderate in spots
- Notes: Beautiful Ocean views, Some Street Walking Necessary; Sunny

BLUFF TOP HIKE

This hike combines bluff top trails with sidewalks and some road side walking. The terrain changes throughout this hike, ranging from improved, wide trails, to sidewalks to footpaths. Please be prepared.

With a little creativity and detouring, this is an enjoyable trip with incredible Ocean views and stretches of flat, easy walking. Whenever possible, we take advantage of the numerous bluff top parks and trails along the Coast.

This is wonderful hike that is perfect for accomplishing in stages as there are many places to park, leaving one car at each end. It is a fun goal to complete and kids thoroughly enjoy the views and the convenient detours here and there down to the beach.

View along Bluff Top Trail

Segment 1: Malaga Cove to Lunada Beach (Distance 3.2 miles)

From Malaga Cove behind the school tower, walk south along Paseo Del Mar. Passing by Bluff Cove, head up the hill and continue right down Paseo Del Mar as it dead ends here. A partially paved footpath extends from its end providing a short cut to Palos Verdes Drive West. In less than a mile you are off Palos Verdes Drive West and are back onto the less traveled Paseo Del Mar heading towards Lunada Bay. Much of this leg can be walked well away from the road on the footpaths along the top of the bluffs.

Segment 2: Lunada Bay to Point Vicente Interpretive Center (Distance 3.7 miles)

From Lunada Bay, walk around the canyon by Via Anacapa and head back toward the bluffs along Paseo Del Mar. Two more very nice, undeveloped and unnamed parks are on this stretch. At the end of Paseo Del Mar is Via Caleta which has an alley that leads back up to Palos Verdes Drive West. After 1/10th of a mile on Palos Verdes Drive West turn down Marguerite Drive. At its end is a gate that is usually unlocked for Pedestrians Only. Pass through it into Oceanfront Park. Walk along the bluff top path through this park to the Point Vicente Interpretive Center.

Segment 3: Point Vicente Interpretive Center to Trump National Golf Course (Distance 4.5 – 5.0 miles)

Start by walking along the shoulder of Palos Verdes Drive South past Terranea Resort, and turn down the next street, Sea Wolf, and then turn right on Beachview. This leads to Vanderlip Park, high up on the cliff. Follow the bluff top trail until you're forced onto Seacoast Drive, leading once again back to Palos Verdes Drive South. Abalone Cove is next and offers a chance to walk further from the roads. Walking to the bluff top tips of Portuguese and Inspiration Point are worth the short detours. From Inspiration Point you can either walk along the shoulder of Palos Verdes Drive South, drop down into the area of the most active land movement used by the South Bay Archery Club, or walk along the beach for a stretch.

The section of beach from Inspiration Point to Trump National Golf Course is one of the easiest on the coast. Either way, the golf course is next and the bluff top trail passes along this whole property.

Segment 4: Trump National Golf Course to Point Fermin Park (Distance 4 miles)
Start from the bluff top trail along Trump National Golf Course which continues into Shoreline Park at the San Pedro City Line. The trail continues past this park and a row of beach front San Pedro homes, eventually turning onto Warmouth Street. Follow this until it reaches Stargazer Avenue and go left and then right onto Paseo Del Mar. About a half mile of street and sidewalk later you connect with White Point County Park. Take the time to read the numerous bronze plaques lining this bluff top which tell of the area's environment and history. From here, walk along the sidewalk to Point Fermin Lighthouse and Park. Herein ends the bluff top hike. If you wish to complete a R.A.T. Beach to Cabrillo Beach trek, continue past Sunken City and down Pacific Avenue to 40th Street, then to Bluff Place which leads to Cabrillo Beach. This extra leg is about 1 mile long.

Trail 52

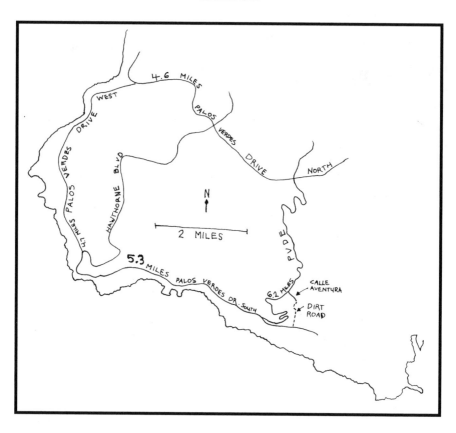

- Distance: 20.8 miles
- Difficulty: Easy to Moderate
- Notes: Loop on Palos Verdes Drives; Different terrains; Busy streets; Popular bike route

PALOS VERDES DRIVE LOOP

This hike is broken up into the four Palos Verdes Drives: North, South, East and West. At some points on this hike you will be on nice improved trails, sometimes dirt footpaths, and at other moments on skinny, bumpy sidewalks next to speeding vehicles. However, this is a hike that many wish to do, just so they can say that they've done it. There is something to be said for having completed this loop: perseverance. The total loop distance is approximately 21 miles.

Palos Verdes Drive North
This stretch has some of the nicest and flattest trails to walk on. For most of its length it actually has 4 paths, one each for cars, bikes, pedestrians and equestrians. The rural feeling of the bridle paths is a wonderful part of life here. Be respectful of the equestrians who use the parallel bridle path and follow the designated trail signs. We begin the loop at the corner of Palos Verdes Drive East, heading west toward Redondo Beach. You can break this trip up in many ways, so we will list some distances for you to make the determination. All of these distances are from the start at Palos Verdes Drive East.
To Rolling Hills Road is 1.1 miles
To Crenshaw Blvd. is 1.7 miles
To Hawthorne Blvd. is 2.2 miles
To Silver Spur is 2.6 miles
To Via Campesina / the City Line is 3.0 miles
Any of these locations can be used to create an intermediate leg on this stretch. At the city line point you can cross over and use the Palos Verdes Drive North Median Trail.   When it ends you will have to cross over to the left side, walking along a light footpath heading up to Malaga Cove Plaza. Here you can cross back over to the right side and the road becomes Palos Verdes Drive West. The total distance of Palos Verdes Drive North is 4.6 miles.

Palos Verdes Drive West

This 4.7 mile stretch from Malaga Cove Plaza to Hawthorne Blvd. has cool ocean breezes all year round. The views along this stretch make the common need to walk along the shoulder worthwhile. The first 1.7 mile section, from Malaga Cove Plaza to the Scenic Viewpoint at Paseo Del Mar, is the worst of it for hiking as you will be walking uphill along a thin shoulder with speeding cars going past. After this you can cross over to the Palos Verdes Drive West Median Trail which is quite nice and flat. Some distances are listed below in case you would like to break up this stretch into smaller sections.

To Palos Verdes Little League Field from the start is 2.3 miles
To Paseo Lunado Parkway is 2.7 miles
At the city line between Palos Verdes Estates and Rancho Palos Verdes the median trail ends. Cross over here to the dirt path along the right side of the road. It soon turns into sidewalk which continues to Hawthorne Blvd., where Palos Verdes Drive West ends.

Palos Verdes Drive South

This coastal stretch offers many beautiful views and is a distance of 6.5 miles. Starting from Hawthorne, the hike begins with sidewalk which dwindles down to a dirt footpath. The trail will alternate between these two as you hike along this hilly stretch. The mileage to resting, or stopping, spots are listed below and are calculated from the start at Hawthorne Blvd.

To Terranea Resort & Spa is 1.1 miles
To Abalone Cove is 3.1 miles
To Portuguese Bend Club is 4.8 miles
To Trump National Golf Course is 5.3 miles
On the Trump property you will have your choice of an improved trail or the sidewalk, and there are lookout points along the way. The distance of Palos Verdes Drive South, ending at Palos Verdes Drive East, is 4.7 miles total.

However, as Palos Verdes Drive East is unsafe to hike up, due to its extremely narrow shoulder and blind corners, continue along Palos Verdes Drive South past the Rancho Palos Verdes / San Pedro city line, to the dirt road heading uphill towards Friendship Park, an additional .6 of a mile.

Palos Verdes Drive East
The switchback section of Palos Verdes Drive East is almost never walked, as there is little to no shoulder, and no trail or sidewalk until the very upper section. The route to bypass this stretch, which is used by many hiking clubs, is to walk up the dirt patrol road leading up into Friendship Park from Palos Verdes Drive South. It is located just past Shoreline Park and the city line and you will need to cross over to the left side of the street. The first ten feet are a little difficult, but it soon moderates into a steady, but steep, uphill walk. At the top of Friendship Park, pass through the gate on your left and walk up along Calle Aventura to connect with Palos Verdes Drive East. Views here are of the Harbor and Ocean and are quite wonderful. The remainder of the trip has a curbside trail or sidewalk that although narrow, is commonly used. Some distances, from Palos Verdes Drive South, along this hike are as follows:
To top of Friendship Park is less than ¾ mile
To Palos Verdes Drive East reconnect is 1 mile
To Miraleste Plaza is 2.2 miles
From here, the hike then begins to head downhill back to Palos Verdes Drive North. The distance to Bronco Drive is 3.5 miles and the full leg distance of Palos Verdes Drive East with the route through Friendship Park is 5.2 miles.

Trail 53

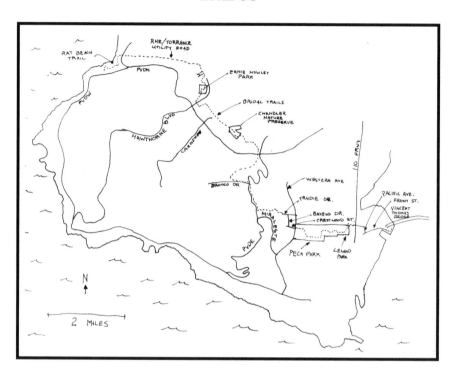

- Distance: North Route – 13 mile trip
- Difficulty: Difficult
- Notes: Linking separate trails; some street walking

Trail 54

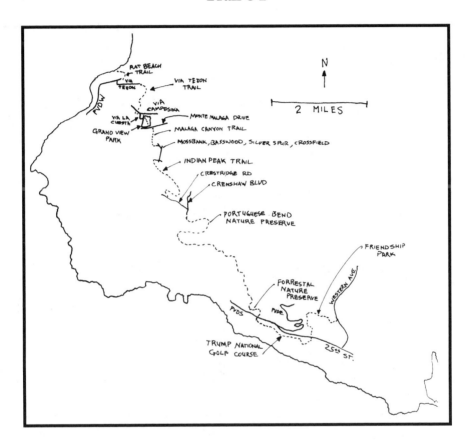

- Distance: South Route – 7 mile trip
- Difficulty: Difficult
- Notes: Linking separate trails; some street walking

TRANS-PENINSULA ROUTES

All trans-peninsula routes involve some street walking. The following two routes minimize this, as much as possible, in favor of open space, park and trail walking. To do this, both of these routes link many of the separate trails within this book into one long hike, going from one side of the Peninsula to the other. It is very helpful and recommended to walk the individual segments before trying to link them for the first time, paying close attention at the ends where the connections are made.

Trans-Peninsula North Route: Malaga Cove to Berth 94 (SS Lane Victory under the Vincent Thomas Bridge)
Distance – 13 miles
Starting from Malaga Cove, behind the school, walk on Malaga Cove Trail to St. Paul's Episcopal Church parking lot. Head out the driveway and cross Palos Verdes Boulevard to the RHE / Torrance Utility Road. This dirt trail goes straight approximately 2 miles to an area overlooking the Torrance Airport. Follow this trail description to negotiate three short blocks of street back to dirt trails and Ernie Howlett Park. Exit at the far side of the park, between the baseball and tennis courts. Go left onto the bridle trails picking your own route from the big map or follow the trail bordering Palos Verdes Drive North for the most direct route. At Palos Verdes Drive East, head up George F Canyon via the Stein-Hale Nature Trail. Continue on the footpath extending from the end of the official trail. This path leads to Bronco Drove. Turn left down the hill, then right onto Palos Verdes Drive East. Miraleste Plaza is in 1 1/4 miles. Walk behind the bus stop and pick up the Miraleste Canyon Trail. Use the Trudie Drive exit off of the trail and head down the street to Bayend Drive. Turn right and go 3 blocks to Crestwood Street. Turn left and head down to Western Avenue. Cross Western Avenue and enter Peck Park. Head South paralleling Western into the Canyon via the paved path. Once on the far side, walk down the canyon all the way through Peck Park and Leland Park. Once on the far side of Gaffey, walk down the trail at the North end of Leland Park leading down to the 110 freeway underpass. Walk along Pacific Avenue to the right

then left on Front Street, which leads to the entrance to the Lane Victory (Berth 94) beneath the Vincent Thomas Bridge.

Trans-Peninsula South Central Route: Friendship Park to Malaga Cove

Distance – 7 miles

The TPSC starts from the Friendship Park parking lot. Start by walking through the park and exiting via the patrol road on the West side of the property. Follow this downhill to 25th Street. Go right to Forrestal Drive. Head right up Forrestal and continue past the yellow gate. Go left down Intrepid Drive and then continue onto the Purple Sage Trail down to the lower section of the Portuguese Bend Nature Preserve. Follow Crenshaw, the prominent dirt road, up to the top. Continue as it becomes the paved street of Crenshaw Blvd. and go one mile to Crestridge Road. Go left on Crestridge to Indian Peak Trail. It cuts over the Hill, coming near Indian Peak Road and Crossfield Drive. Follow Crossfield Drive to Silver Spur Road and go left. Take Basswood Avenue left and then Mossbank Drive left to Malaga Canyon Trail, which originates from the end of Mossbank Drive. Take this down to Montemalaga Drive. Go left to Grayslake Road, go right, then left onto Ironwood Street. Pass through Grandview Park and cross over the top. On the far side of the park, take Via La Cuesta down (left) to Via Campesina (left). Next connect with the Via Tejon Trail at the entrance of the paved Del Sol Fire Road. Continue on Via Tejon Trail until it ends at Via Tejon Road. Follow Via Tejon Road across Palos Verdes Drive West then go left and head down Via Corta to the parking lot, behind the school.

Frascati Canyon

Chapter 4

Median Trails & More

There are great walks that can be done just along walkways, sidewalks and median trails, and we have listed our favorites in this chapter. Many are beautifully landscaped by the cities and are mostly wide and flat. Although walking close to a busy street might take away from the rural feel of the area, the Ocean views, convenience and easy walking might just make up for it.

We felt it beneficial to list two sidewalk sections as they can be used on their own or to connect from one park or trail area to another. The locations listed, Palos Verdes Drive East/Narbonne and Palos Verdes Drive North, have three things in common: good length; separation from the busy road they parallel and a nice rural feel.

The waterfront walkway along Harbor Boulevard, officially referred to as a parkway, is all new and very nice. It is beautiful at night and viewing the ships up close as they head out to sea, is quite a remarkable experience.

Median Trails, Sidewalks & Parkway

55) Harbor Boulevard Parkway/Ports O'Call
56) Miraleste Median Trail
57) Paseo la Cresta Median Trail
58) Palos Verdes Drive East/Narbonne Sidewalk
59) Palos Verdes Drive North Median Trail
60) Palos Verdes Drive North Sidewalk
61) Palos Verdes Drive West Median Trail

HARBOR BOULEVARD PARKWAY / PORTS O'CALL BOARDWALK
Trail 55
The nicely designed and landscaped waterfront walkway along the Harbor in San Pedro is the first leg of a planned walkway from the bridge to the breakwall. It is beautifully lit at night and monitored by video surveillance to help keep it clean and safe. A variety of artwork, walking surfaces, and informative stops keep the walk interesting. As an added benefit, the Red Car Trolleys run alongside the walkway providing cheap, easy and fun transportation back to your car, should you want it. The north end of the walkway begins close to the entrance of the SS Lane Victory under the Vincent Thomas Bridge. So far, the new parkway extends to the Fire Boathouse near the Los Angeles Maritime Museum. You can easily continue on the sidewalk from here, past the museum, and connect with the boardwalk of Ports O'Call where there are many shops and restaurants.

MIRALESTE DRIVE MEDIAN TRAIL
Trail 56
This mostly shady trail starts at Palos Verdes Drive East and ends at Via Colinita. Most of the trail is improved and flat, although there are short footpath sections and some up and down. There are canyon trails all around this median trail to create loop hikes if desired.

PASEO LA CRESTA MEDIAN TRAIL
Trail 57
This landscaped improved trail travels in the middle of the split road Paseo la Cresta. It is mostly used by local residents jogging or dog walking. The trail extends between Via Chispas and Via Fernandez. Crossing the street connects to a nice landscaped park area at the Via Fernandez end. Paseo la Cresta is a mostly sunny trail with some trees and wonderful ocean views.

PALOS VERDES DRIVE EAST / NARBONNE
Trail 58
This sidewalk starts at the corner of Palos Verdes Drive North and ends across the street from the Lomita Sheriff Department near the Rolling Hills Estates/Lomita border. This mostly shady, trail runs slightly downhill and is separated from the road by plants and a white fence intermittently. The trail is shared in sections by equestrians, so please give them right away. Behind the sheriff station is a dirt utility road which goes two blocks west.

PALOS VERDES DRIVE NORTH MEDIAN TRAIL
Trail 59
This shady, crushed gravel trail travels in the middle of the split section of Palos Verdes Drive North in Palos Verdes Estates. It is regularly used by local residents out for an evening stroll, a jog or walking the dog. The trail extends between Via Valmonte and Via Pasqual and is approximately 1 mile long.

PALOS VERDES DRIVE NORTH SIDEWALK
Trail 60
This shady sidewalk area from the corner of Palos Verdes Drive East to Via Valmonte is a wonderful stretch. There are plenty of shady spots and the sidewalk parallels a Bridle Trail away from the road. Please be respectful of the Bridle Trail and stay only on the pedestrian path. At the PV Drive East end you can connect to the Palos Verdes Drive East/Narbonne sidewalk, the Reservoir Trail or the George F Canyon Trail. At the Via Valmonte end you can connect to the Palos Verdes Drive North Median Trail listed just above.

PALOS VERDES DRIVE WEST MEDIAN TRAIL
Trail 61
The crushed gravel improved trail begins at the scenic overlook at
Paso Del Mar. The median trail stops at the Paseo Lunado grass park
and then quickly continues until the Palos Verdes / Rancho Palos
Verdes city line. The trail has sunny areas and trees for shade, as
well as some Ocean views.

Palos Verdes Drive North

Chapter 5

Get Looped for Lunch

After repeated requests, we get it, people love loops - especially
those with a fun stop along the way. So, the following hikes are
presented with just this idea in mind.

We have put together five loops that combine different trails and
offer a wonderful spot to stop and enjoy something to eat at one of
the local restaurants or markets. Now, what did you think we meant
by looped?

Palos Verdes Drive East / Narbonne

Trail 62

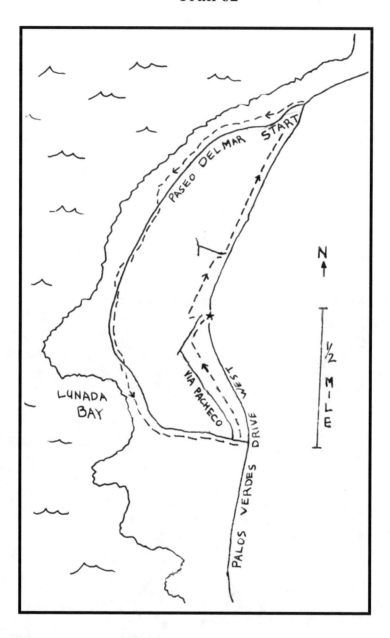

- Distance: Approximately 4 mile round trip
- Difficulty: Easy
- Notes: Sunny; some street walking

LUNADA LUNCH LOOP

Start from the scenic overlook and parking lot at the beginning of Paseo Del Mar as it cuts off from Palos Verdes Drive West. Follow the Bluff Top Trail south. The path alternates from a bluff top dirt path to street walking along Paseo Del Mar. Follow the road when it bends left away from the Ocean and becomes Paseo Lunado. You can walk along the improved trail in the grassy median here if desired.

Right after passing Via Pecheco and before connecting with Palos Verdes Drive West, there is a very short paved driveway which immediately becomes a dirt trail under the telephone wires that heads back north. Follow this trail heading back toward Lunada Bay. At Via Bandini, the trail becomes a paved alley. Continue along until Via Anacapa or the next street, Yarmouth Road, either of which take you to restaurant and market choices if you turn right.

When you are finished, continue back down the alley which soon becomes a dirt trail again. The path ends at Dalton Road. From here, just turn right on Dalton and connect with Palos Verdes Drive West and its median trail. Follow the median trail until it reaches the beginning of Paseo Del Mar. Cross Palos Verdes Drive West and you are back at your vehicle.

Trail 63

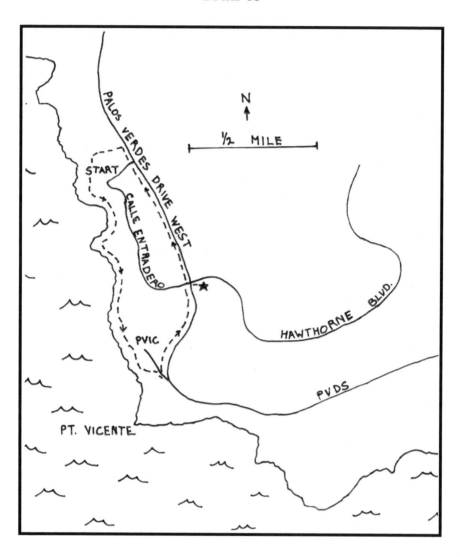

- Distance: Approximately 2 miles
- Difficulty: Easy to moderate
- Notes: Sunny; Ocean views

LOFTY LOOP

Start at the parking lot of Oceanfront Park off of Calle Entradero. Head out on the Oceanfront Park Trail, right off the parking lot, towards the Palos Verdes Interpretive Center. Follow this trail along the bluff top route and cross the bridge that connects to the PVIC's bluff top trail. Continue along the length of the property and when the trail ends at the Coast Guard property fence, head through the parking lot to the sidewalk on Palos Verdes Drive South. Stay on the ocean side of Palos Verdes Drive South here and follow the sidewalk up to the left, looking back over the Oceanfront Park area. Cross the street at Hawthorne Blvd. and enjoy a number of wonderful choices for food or coffee with ocean views and outdoor seating.

When finished, head back across the street at Hawthorne Blvd. Walk right along Palos Verdes Drive South which is now, since crossing Hawthorne Blvd., Palos Verdes Drive West. This is a nice improved trail and although it is along a busy street, the view is wonderful. Continue walking just past Calle Entradero and there is a marked entrance on your left to a dirt path that heads down to the bluff top. This dirt path connects you to the Oceanfront parking lot where you started.

Trail 64

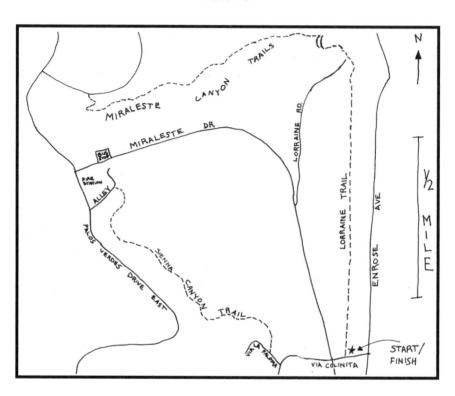

- Distance: Approximately 3 miles
- Difficulty: Easy
- Notes: Mostly shady

LOOP de MIRALESTE

Although there are many options here, we have chosen one of the longest combinations that also remains mostly on trails, not streets. Start on the Lorraine Road Trail and then connect with the Miraleste Canyon Trails. Cross the bridge to the other side of Miraleste Canyon and hike up the canyon. When the dirt trail ends and connects with the street, turn left and walk to Palos Verdes Drive East and take another left. Head across Miraleste Drive where there is a restaurant and market available in the plaza area.

When you are ready to head out again, start down the alley to connect with Sienna Canyon Trails. Turn down the right trail and follow down the canyon. When you hit the street, head down to the left toward Via Colinita. Cross Miraleste Drive and you are back at the start.

Trail 65

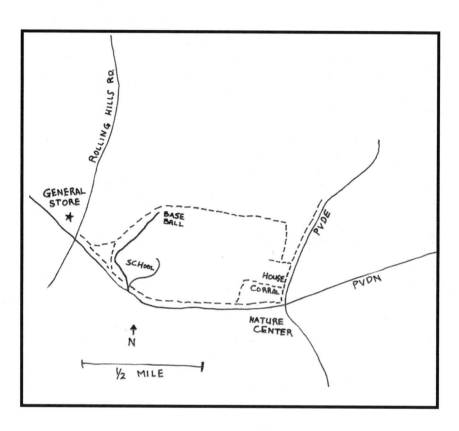

- Distance: 2 ¼ miles
- Difficulty: Easy
- Notes: Bridle trail hiking – give right of way to equestrians

LAME HORSE LOOP

This is a simple loop starting and ending at the George F Canyon Nature Center and leading to The General Store and Kelly's Korner.

Start from the Nature Center at the corner of Palos Verdes Drive North and East. Walk downhill (north) on Palos Verdes Drive East and turn left onto the second bridle trail just past the corral and one house. Follow this trail as it branches quickly to the right, skirting along the golf course. The trail turns to the left and in a ¼ mile leads through Chandler Nature Preserve. Turn left, uphill, on the dirt bridle trail past the baseball diamond. At the Y in the trail head right again uphill. The trail soon runs parallel to Palos Verdes Drive North. Cross Rolling Hills Road to the General Store.

The easy return is to the left, back along the separate sidewalk next to Palos Verdes Drive North. Cross over at the intersection with PV Drive East and you are back at the Nature Center.

Still full of energy? Hike the up and back Stein/Hale Trail heading out from the Nature Center or do the Reservoir Loop just across PV Drive East.

Trail 66

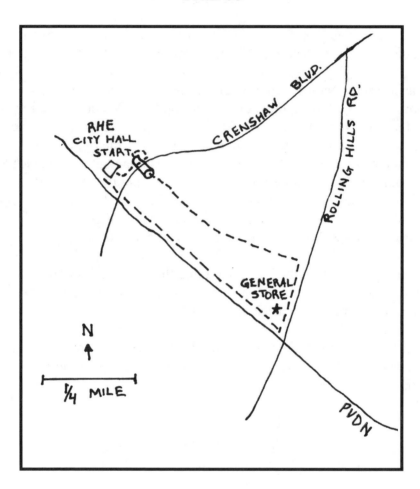

- Distance: 1 ½ miles round trip
- Difficulty: Easy
- Notes: Some bridle trail hiking – give right of way to equestrians

LANDMARK LOOP

This loop starts at Rolling Hills Estates City Hall and the suggested stop halfway is the General Store and Kelly's Korner. From city hall walk downhill on Crenshaw (do not cross street) and turn into the first opening in the fence past the private Seahorse Riding Academy. Walk to the end of the short stretch of white fence. Do a U turn around the fence down onto the Botanical Gardens Bridle Trail and pass through the tunnel under Crenshaw Blvd. Follow this straight trail to Rolling Hills Road. Turn right uphill and the General Store will be quickly on your right. Enjoy a nice break with lunch and/or ice cream outside.

When you are ready to head back, walk along the separate sidewalk area along Palos Verdes Drive North. It is nice and shady for most of this walk. There is a separate bridle trail running parallel to the sidewalk, so please make sure to stay on the area designated for pedestrians. Cross over Crenshaw Blvd. at the corner and you are back at the beginning.

The Points from Hawthorne Blvd.

Chapter 6

Bridle Trail Rules

The Bridle Trails are a unique part of the Peninsula's heritage, and they are extensive, covering a large part of the Hill. Some of the prominent ones have been included with the hiking trails in the previous chapters and described as part of the areas where they originate as well as mentioned to link one area to another. If you would like a complete listing of the bridle trails, we would definitely recommend picking up a copy of the Palos Verdes Peninsula Horsemen's Association Trail Guide, which focuses on the bridle trails specifically.

Most of the bridle trails shown on our maps can be used by hikers and pedestrians. That being said, they were built by, are maintained by, and primarily meant to be used by equestrians. Use by others should be done with the courtesy of a guest.

<u>The rules for hikers using the bridle trails are:</u>

- No motorized vehicles of any kind on any trail
- No smoking on bridle trails
- Dogs must be on a leash and under control at all times
- Stay on trails – respect private property
- Equestrians always have right of way – stop, get out of their way, let them pass
- Do not try to touch a horse, walk behind them, or make loud or sudden moves around them
- Say hello to riders in a normal tone of voice, and when passing a horse from behind stay 25 feet back until the rider clears you to pass
- Walk calmly past horses, remember they can sometimes be unpredictictable or dangerous
- Bicycles are not allowed on the Rolling Hills and Rolling Hills Estates Bridle Trails
- The entire city of Rolling Hills is private property

The Peninsula offers a wonderful opportunity for people with many different interests to use the same outdoor areas. If we are respectful to each other, this will hopefully always be the case.

Bluff Top in Lunada Bay

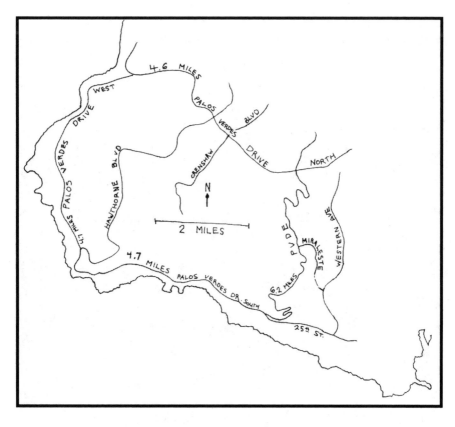

- Distance: PVDN = 4.6 miles; PVDW = 4.7 miles;
  PVDS = 4.7 miles; PVDE = 6.2 miles;
  Hawthorne = 5.9 miles; Crenshaw = 2.2
  miles; Crest = 1.7 miles
- Difficulty: Difficult
- Notes: These routes are rated difficult due to
  the extremely narrow shoulders along
  most of these streets

Chapter 7

Bikeways

Street Routes

The streets on the Peninsula are windy, narrow and most have very little shoulder. Palos Verdes Drive North and Palos Verdes Drive South are the streets with the best bike routes along their shoulders. Palos Verdes Drive East has signs posted stating "Warning: Not Suitable For Bicycles". Caution should be exercised by everyone using these streets as accidents between bicyclists and motorists have happened here. For many, joining a bicycle club may provide better understanding of the conditions and hazards inherent to street riding, as well as providing a friendlier and safer way to explore the beauty and diversity of this area from the intimacy of a bicycle seat. One local organization is the South Bay Wheelmen found at southbaywheelmen.org . The popular route forming a loop of Palos Verdes Drive North, East, South, and west is approximately 20 miles. For a complete description of the Palos Verdes Drive Loop see that title in Chapter 7. Hawthorne, Crenshaw, Rolling Hills Road, Crest and Miraleste are also commonly used to create different loops.

Off-Road Routes

This book was primarily written with hikers in mind, but most of the trails in this book are also open to bikes. Keep in mind that bridle trails are off limits to bikes. The entire city of Rolling Hills is off limits to all off-road bikers. Additionally signs are posted in many individual areas stating no bikes, especially in some Ecological and Nature Preserves. Remember freedom comes with responsibility. Downhill riders give right of way to uphill riders. All bikers give right of way to equestrians.

The making of jumps and bank turns is in most cases illegal, especially in most Preserves.

CORBA, Concerned Off-Road Bicyclists Association, has a local Palos Verdes chapter. Their goal is to keep the trails open to bicyclists by educating off-road cyclists about trail etiquette and the natural habitats surrounding the trails. Their website is mtbpv.org and email is info@mtbpv.org.

Portuguese Bend Nature Preserve

Chapter 8

Going the Extra Mile

If you enjoy this area as much as we do, and you want to show your concern in a meaningful way, there are several things you can do almost every time you hike.

First, the easiest thing to do is to simply pick up the trash and litter left behind by others. We practice this and in so doing have acquired an impressive collection of old bottles for our garage, many of them dating back decades.

Second, you can be respectful of areas where there is new planting. These areas are especially sensitive. Keeping your children, dog, horse and even yourself clear of the flags and milk cartons used to mark and protect these young plants, is greatly appreciated.

Third, you can volunteer with local organizations which work diligently to keep the Peninsula a special place to live. Some organizations are involved with protecting and improving native habitats by weeding and planting; some are involved with educating the public about the land and its history; others work to maintain and dedicate local land as trails, parks, open space or nature preserves. The Palos Verdes Peninsula Land Conservancy (www.pvplc.org) is the most active organization focused on Peninsula land and offers a diversity of volunteering opportunities. A full list of organizations on the hill is located in Chapter 10. If you are interested in volunteering, there is definitely an organization that can offer an opportunity to fit your interest.

Highridge Park

Chapter 9

Parks & Points of Interest

Abalone Cove Shoreline State Marine Park
5907 PV Drive South, Rancho Palos Verdes, CA 90275
310-377-1222
This park has an open space area with picnic tables throughout its
bluff top field. Hike down the path to access two different beaches:
Abalone Cove and Sacred Cove. The sandy shoreline found here is
nice for walking or relaxing and the tide pools are great for
exploring. It is a State Ecological Preserve so taking of plants or
animals is illegal and no dogs are allowed. From here most of the
south side of the peninsula can be explored by foot or bicycle. There
is a $5.00 parking fee.

Angel's Gate Cultural Center
3601 South Gaffey Street, San Pedro, California 90731
angelsgateart.org ; 310-519-0936
The Center offers classes and exhibits to the community throughout
the year. Work areas are also provided here for over 50 artists. The
Angel Gate Shop offers local art for sale to the public.

Angel's Gate Lighthouse
This historic lighthouse is located at the end of the 9,250 foot long
breakwater and marks the entrance to the Los Angeles Harbor. It has
an interesting history and original design that is worth seeing by boat.
Many people walk along the breakwater, although the sections that
have been repaired are difficult to traverse and waves have swept
people off of the rocks.

Angel's Gate Recreation Center & Park
3601 South Gaffey Street, San Pedro, CA 90731
310-548-7705
This 64 acre park offers a beautiful grass lawn area with a children's
playground, basketball court, soccer field and a recreation center.
The views from here are breathtaking. The Korean Friendship Bell,
Fort MacArthur Military Museum, the Marine Mammal Care Center
and the International Bird Rescue Center are located here.
(All four are included in this list alphabetically.)

Averill Park
1300 South Dodson Avenue, San Pedro, CA 90732
310-548-7671
This is a beautiful vintage park with a shady stream and sunny grass
hillsides on either side. There is a pond full of ducks and geese at the
stream's lower end. There are picnic tables scattered throughout and
a gazebo on the hilltop. The incredible views here are of the Harbor.

Banning Residence Museum
401 East M Street, Wilmington, CA 90744
www.banningmuseum.org ; 310-548-7777
General Phineas Banning was one of the founders of Los Angeles
and instrumental in the building of the Los Angeles Harbor. His
residence was built in 1864 and the 90 minute tours offered at the
museum cover this extraordinary building and more. The museum is
situated on a 20 acre lawn park which is popular with bird watchers.

Bogdanovich Recreation Center & Park
1920 Cumbre Drive, San Pedro, CA 90732
bogdanovichrc@rap.lacity.org; 310-548-7590
The Bogdanovich Recreation Center sits atop a hill surrounded by
the 123 acre Friendship Park. Its parking lot can be accessed from
Cumbre Drive or from 9th Street, but is closest to Cumbre Drive.
There are baseball and soccer fields, picnic tables, restrooms, a large
children's play area, indoor basketball courts and a bocci ball area
located here.

Cabrillo Beach
Stephen M White Drive, San Pedro, CA 90731
There is a gate as you enter the parking lot; the fee is $6.00. Cabrillo
Beach actually has two beaches: one outside the breakwall, exposed
to the surf, and the other inside the Harbor with no waves. The inner
beach has a playground for children and a fishing pier for a nice
stroll. On the far left, is a boat landing area and bird sanctuary
(Salinas de San Pedro).

Cabrillo Beach Bathhouse
3800 Stephen White Drive, San Pedro, CA 90731
310-548-7554   www.cabrillobeachbathhouse.org
The 26,000 square foot building was the last bathhouse to be built in
Southern California in 1932 and is located at Cabrillo Beach. There
are classes offered here to the community and changing exhibits. Call
for more information.

Cabrillo Marina
Via Cabrillo Marina, San Pedro, CA 90731
Walk along the sidewalks surrounding this marina and enjoy looking at some beautiful boats. There are restaurants along the way to stop and relax with a nice cool beverage.

Cabrillo Marine Aquarium
3720 Stephen White Drive, San Pedro, CA 90731
www.cabrilloaq.org ; 310-548-7562
Cabrillo Marine Aquarium is an aquatic exhibition facility that the whole family will learn from and enjoy. It is located just across the parking lot from Cabrillo Beach. There are over 35 saltwater aquariums and a wonderful touch tank. Contact them for information on special events and what children's programs they are currently running.

Chandler Park
Corner of Crenshaw Blvd. & PV Drive North,
Rolling Hills Estates, CA 90274
This 20 acre grassy park has a corral and access to the bridle trails. Located behind the Rolling Hills Estates City Hall, it is used mainly by equestrians and dog owners. There are benches and a wheel chair accessible port-a-potti. In the back corner is a drinking fountain for horses only.

Clovercliff Park
28801 Golden Meadow Drive, Rancho Palos Verdes, CA 90275
This tiny, quiet and shady park is located in a small lot between houses. It has a little path and is landscaped.

Deane Dana Friendship Park Nature Center
1850 W. 9th Street, San Pedro, CA 90732
310-519-6115   go to www.sanpedrochamber.com to get link
Deane Dana Nature Center is part of the 123 acre Friendship Park. Its parking lot is on the north side of the entrance road and adjacent to that of the Bogdanovich Recreation Center. This park has large grass lawns, many types of trails, a children's playground, picnic tables

and restrooms. The Nature Center has a museum and offers children's story time, and guided birdwalks as well as many other special events. Contact the center for more information.

Del Cerro Park
#2 Park Place, Rancho Palos Verdes, CA 90275
There is a large grass area here with a wood fence around the perimeter. The park offers views of the Portuguese Bend area as well as the Ocean and Catalina Island beyond. There is a drinking fountain and parking lot convenient to the Portuguese Bend Nature Preserve.

Drum Barracks Civil War Museum
1052 North Banning Avenue, Wilmington, CA 97044
www.drumbarracks.org 310-548-7509
The Drum Barracks is the only U.S. Army building still standing from the Civil War. The museum contains many historical artifacts and there are tours available. Call for tour availability.

Eastview Park
1700 Westmont Avenue, San Pedro, CA
Walk uphill to the park, from the parking lot, on either the footpath on the left or on the improved trail on the right. This 9.9 acre park includes a large grassy area, a children's playground, a jogging path and restrooms.

Ernie Howlett Park
25852 Hawthorne Blvd., Rolling Hills Estates, CA 90274
310-541-4585
This park has a large grassy area with picnic benches, a children's playground and tennis courts on the left as you enter. Behind the parking lot is a large grassy area with a baseball diamond. There are equestrian stables surrounding the area, corrals and access to extensive bridle paths.

Fort MacArthur Military Museum
(Battery Osgood-Farley Historic Site)
3601 S. Gaffey Street, San Pedro, CA 90731
www.ftmax.org ; 310-548-2631
Fort MacArthur was a U.S. Army post which guarded the Los
Angeles Harbor from 1914 to 1974. The Museum, created in 1985,
is located in the corridors and galleries of historic Battery Osgood-
Farley. Includes extensive local history.

Founders Park
1 Ocean Trails Dr., Rancho Palos Verdes, CA 90275;
310-265-5000
www.palosverdes.com/RPV/recreationparks/Founders/index.cfm
Founders Park is located behind the Trump National Clubhouse. It is
an open grass area with picnic tables and a gazebo. The park has
plaques telling the history of the area and wonderful Ocean views.

Frank A. Vanderlip, Sr. Park
6500 Seacove, Rancho Palos Verdes, CA 90275
This .48 acre park has a walkway and benches to sit and enjoy the
Pacific Ocean and Island views.

Fred Hesse Jr. Community Park
29301 Hawthorne Blvd., Rancho Palos Verdes, CA 90275
310-541-8114
The landscaped upper park has soccer and baseball fields, picnic
benches with barbecues, a quarter mile walkway and three children's
play areas. The lower park area shows a more natural habitat with
trails, picnic tables, benches and a sand volleyball court. This park
area surrounds a community center which offers a variety of classes
and services for the public.

Friendship Park
1850 W. 9ᵗʰ Street, San Pedro, CA 90732   310-519-6115
see: Deana Dana Friendship Park Nature Center

The General Store
26947 Rolling Hills Way, RHE, 90274   310-541-3668
An established Peninsula landmark. A long time destination for
equestrians as many Bridle trails connect here. Stop and enjoy lunch
at Kelly's Korner before heading on your way.

George F Canyon Nature Center
Corner of PV Drive East & PV Drive North, RHE, 90274
310-547-0862
The Nature Center, at the beginning of the Stein/Hale Nature Trail,
has live animals, bones, and other nature exhibits for kids to explore
as well nature-themed kids' gifts and activites. Contact the center for
children's story times, guided hikes, bird walks and special events.

Harbor Boulevard Parkway
Along Harbor Blvd., Swinford St. to 5th Street, San Pedro
www.sanpedrowaterfront.com
This waterfront promenade has palm trees, benches, chess and
backgammon tables, a bocci ball court, a variety of artwork and
plaques commemorating the history of the area. The walkway
parallels the Red Car trolley route (see Waterfront Red Car Line).
This is just the beginning of the Parkway, as it is projected to extend
to Cabrillo Beach thereby completing the motto "Bridge to
Breakwater".

Highridge Park
29035 Highridge Road, Rolling Hills Estates, CA 90274
This park has soccer and baseball fields. Off of the parking lot is a
children's playground with picnic benches and restrooms. There is a
par fitness course by the baseball fields and access to the bridle trails.

International Bird Rescue & Research Center
3601 S. Gaffey Street, at Leavenworth Drive, San Pedro, CA 90731
ibrrc.org; 310-514-2573
This center rescues shore birds, migrating waterfowl and sea birds.
This facility is not generally open to the public, but volunteer
opportunities available. Call for more information.

Joan Milke Flores Park
3601 S. Gaffey Street, San Pedro, CA 90731
(enter off of Paseo Del Mar)
This park has a large grass lawn with picnic benches and ample parking. It is located across the street from Point Fermin Lighthouse Park and connects to Angel's Gate Park/Fort MacArthur. See: Fort MacArthur Trails.

Ken Malloy Harbor Regional Park
15820 S. Vermont Avenue, Harbor City, CA 90710
310-548-7728; KMHarbor.RegionalPark@lacity.org
This park area has a large lake with extensive bird life. There is a children's playground, picnic areas, and restrooms. You can walk around most of the lake on paved and dirt paths and there are very large, open grass lawns.

Knoll Hill Off-Leash Dog Park
On Knoll Drive – East of Pacific Avenue
310-514-0338
The entrance to this park is located on Front Road just off of Pacific Avenue. This is a fenced area for dogs to run free off-leash. It is located on top of Knoll Hill in San Pedro.

Korean Bell of Friendship & Bell Pavilion
Angels Gate Park, Gaffey and 37th Street, San Pedro 90731
The Korean bell and pavilion was donated in 1976 to the people of Los Angeles by the people of the Republic of Korea. The gift was to celebrate the United State's bicentennial, to honor veterans of the Korean War, and to consolidate friendship between the two countries. The Pavilion is located in Angel's Gate Park.

Leland Recreation Center & Park
863 S. Herbert Avenue, San Pedro, CA 90731
310-548-7706
This park has outdoor sports fields, a basketball court and picnic benches. The active center offers classes and programs for children and adults and a community room for public use.

Ladera Linda Park & Discovery Room
32201 Forrestal Drive, Rancho Palos Verdes, CA 90275
310-541-7073
This multi-level area is bordered by the Forrestal Nature Preserve. As you enter the first parking lot, there is a children's playground, basketball courts, grassy area and Discovery Room. If you drive through the lower part to the upper parking lot there is another children's playground, two paddle ball courts and a grassy area with a picnic bench. If you follow the steps up to the third area, there are soccer and baseball fields belonging to the local school district. All three areas have fantastic views of Catalina Island. The Discovery Room in the Community Center features exhibits of animals and plants of the local area. Bathrooms are located in the Community Center as well.

Los Angeles Harbor Fire Station #112
638 S. Beacon Street, San Pedro, CA 90731
www.lafire.com/fire_boats
This building was designed to hold Fire Boat #2, the Ralph Scott. There are exhibits here on the history of the Ralph Scott and also on Fire Boats in Los Angeles.

Los Angeles Maritime Museum
Berth 84, Harbor Blvd. & 6th Street, San Pedro, CA 90731
www.maritimemuseum.org ; 310-548-7618
This 75,000 square foot building holds the largest maritime museum in all of California. Full of history, the museum has everything from interesting ship models inside to the real ships anchored outside. Cost is $3 for adults and children are free.

Madrona Marsh Preserve & Nature Center
3201 Plaza Del Amo, Torrance, CA 90274
310-782-3989; www.freindsofmadronamarsh.com
The Nature Center is an educational and interpretive site that hosts an Exhibit Hall and Laboratory. There is information available on all aspects of the marsh and its plant and animal life. A variety of classes and programs are offered for the local community through the Center and information on guided hikes is available here as well.

Malaga Cove Museum & Farnham Martins Park

2400 Via Campesina, Palos Verdes, CA 90274
The Art Museum is on the lower floor of the Malaga Cove Library
and can be accessed through the library or a separate entrance on Via
Campesina. It hosts art exhibits that change periodically and the
hours are the same as the library. The Farnham Martins Park, located
next to the building, is a grassy area under large trees with a fountain
area.

Marine Mammal Care Center

www.mar3ine.org; 310-548-5677
3601 S. Gaffey Street, at Leavenworth Drive, San Pedro, CA
This is a hospital for sick or injured seals and sea lions. It is open to
the public to view the animals and their progress. The Center works
with the community offering educational opportunities for schools,
and features exhibits and information on marine mammals. There is
also a gift shop to check out and volunteer opportunities are always
available.

Martingale Trailhead Park
22 Martingale Drive, Rancho Palos Verdes, CA 90275
This tiny park is aptly named as it leads right to trails. It has a beautiful canyon view and a multi-purpose fountain.

Memorials:
American Merchant Marine Veterans Memorial
Fishing Industry Memorial
Liberty Hill Monument
Longshore Memorial
U.S.S. Los Angeles Naval Monument
South Harbor Blvd At West 5th Street, San Pedro, CA 90731
These memorials are located along Harbor Blvd. They have plaques describing their history and connection to the local area.

Muller House Museum
1542 S. Beacon Street, San Pedro, CA 90731
310-831-1788
Built in 1899, this museum is run by the San Pedro Bay Historical Society. It is an example of 1920s living.

Neptune Fountain
Malaga Cove Plaza, PV Drive N., PVE, CA 90274
This fountain is a copy of the original which needed to be replaced in 1968 due to its deterioration. Both statues were created from Italian marble.

Norris Center for the Performing Arts
Includes the Norris Theatre & The Harlyne J. Norris Pavilion
27570 Crossfield Drive, Rolling Hills Estates, CA 90274
www.norristheatre.org ; 310-544-0403
Both buildings offer a theatre, rehearsal areas, meeting rooms for events and offer classes and community outreach programs. The Norris Theatre hosts the Upstairs Gallery with changing art exhibits and the Pavilion is home to the Negri Learning Center.

Palos Verdes Art Center
5504 W. Crestridge Road, Rancho Palos Verdes, CA 90275
www.pvartcenter.org ; 310-541-2479
The newly renovated Art Center holds 3 galleries with changing exhibits. The center works with the community on numerous levels offering a large variety of services and classes to the public. Call for a schedule of upcoming events.

Palos Verdes Estates Parks
There are over 849 acres of parkland owned by PVE. The land is broken into smaller parcels and scattered throughout the city. Some of these are landscaped and nestled within neighborhoods, while others are open space areas. The parks do not offer amenities such as restrooms, picnic tables, children's playground or public parking. As most are unnamed, they are referred to by the streets around them, such as Coronel Plaza, Dolores Plaza, Montemalaga Plaza, Valmonte Plaza, Via Morola Park and Paseo La Cresta Park, to name a few.

Palos Verdes Memorial Garden
Malaga Cove, Palos Verdes, CA 90274
There is a flag memorial here with additional memorials and benches surrounding the center piece. A grassy area surrounds the memorial.

Palos Verdes Estates Shoreline Preserve
Along Paseo Del Mar, Palos Verdes, CA 90274
This bluff top area starts and stops along Paseo Del Mar, beginning at the Scenic Overlook where there is public parking. There is a trail along much of this area and we describe it the Bluff Top Hike in Chapter 3.

Peck Park
Corner of Summerland and Western Blvd., San Pedro, CA
310-548-7580 Rec Ctr; 310-548-2434 Swimming Pool
Driving into Peck Park, off of Western Blvd., one will pass a large grass lawn area, a children's playground, a community center on the right and a gymnasium and tennis courts on the far left. At the

parking lot, a road veers off to the left which leads to more parking for the tennis courts, and to the outdoor public swimming pool. There are also athletic fields here for baseball and soccer, as well as a large canyon to be explored.

Point Fermin Lighthouse

Point Fermin Lighthouse & Park

807 Paseo Del Mar, San Pedro, CA 90731; 310-241-0684
The Victorian Lighthouse was built in 1874 and aided sailors in a safe passage to the Los Angeles Harbor. Today the lighthouse sits in the 37 acre park which has picnic tables, a children's play area, restrooms and a stage for shows. Tours of the lighthouse are available with a history of the light and its keepers.

Point Fermin State Marine Park & Life Refuge

Beach below Point Fermin Park, San Pedro, CA 90731
www.pointferminlighthouse.org
This area is more commonly known as Sunken City and its trail is described in Chapter 4. As it is a Wildlife Refuge, no animals or plants are to be taken from this area.

Point Vicente Interpretive Center

31501 Palos Verdes Drive West, RPV, CA 90275
310-377-5370
The recently expanded Interpretive Center is now 7,000 square feet larger and contains information on the Peninsula and exhibits about the water's inhabitants below. The walkway, along the coast outside of the Center, is known for whale watching, specifically that of the migrating Pacific gray whale, although others are also seen.

Point Vicente Lighthouse

31501 Palos Verdes Drive West, RPV, CA 90275
310-541-0334
The lighthouse, built in 1926, is operated by the U.S. Coastguard and sits on 8 landscaped acres. It is open to the public on the 2nd Saturday of each month from 10 – 3pm (1st Sat. in March). Admission is free.

Ports O'Call Village

End of 6th Street, Past Harbor Blvd., San Pedro, CA 90731
This harbor area covers over 15 acres and houses a wide variety of shops, restaurants, and activities. Here you will find small boats to rent for two, large sailing vessels for private parties, tour boats for informative trips around the Harbor, and much more.

Rancho Palos Verdes City Hall Park / Upper Point Vicente
30940 Hawthorne Blvd., Rancho Palos Verdes, CA 90275
This park has a grassy area, a tennis court and a volleyball area near the RPV City Hall building. If you go to the left as you enter, there is a remote control helicopter area and a large natural field.

Robert E. Ryan Community Park
30359 Hawthorne Boulevard, RPV, CA 90275
310-377-2290
There are three areas of children's playground here and the large grassy field includes a baseball diamond. The small community center has bathrooms and is next to the basketball courts.

Rockbluff Park
Corner of PV Drive North & Hawthorne, Rolling Hills Estates, CA 90274
This park is a large grassy area with a hill at the back of the property. On the upper part there is a playground area for children. There is access here to the bridle trails.

Santa Catalina Island
www.catalina.com ; 310-510-1520
email: info@visitcatalina.org
The Island has two ports on the mainland side: Avalon and Two Harbors. The entire island offers a wide variety of activities, museums and history. Contact the Island or check out their website for travel and lodging information.

Silver Spur Park
Corner of Silver Spur & PV Drive North,
Rolling Hills Estates, CA 90274
This triangularly shaped park is a landscaped grassy area with a bench. It has access to the trails along Palos Verdes Drive North.

Salinas de San Pedro / Cabrillo Aquarium Salt Marsh
Off of Stephen White Drive, San Pedro, CA 90731
Use Cabrillo Aquarium Parking Lot; 310-548-7562
This sanctuary is locked to keep the public from disturbing the animals using the area. The area is managed by the Cabrillo Aquarium and a key can be acquired there in exchange for your driver's license.

South Coast Botanic Garden
26300 Crenshaw Blvd., Rolling Hills Estates, CA 90274
www.southcoastbotanicgarden.org ; 310-544-1948
This 87 acre area contains wonderful walks to a lake with ducks, a garden just for children, a large rose garden with a fountain and an herb garden to mention just a few highlights. There is also a Garden Gift & Plant Shop. Special events and classes are held throughout the year.

SS Lane Victory
Berth 94, San Pedro, 90731
www.lanevictory.org ; 310-519-9545
This fully restored World War II cargo ship is located at the North end of the new Harbor Boulevard Parkway. There is a museum and gift shop on board and tours are available. The ship also heads out to sea periodically. Call for dates and tickets.

Waterfront Red Car Line
Runs along Harbor Blvd., at the waterfront, San Pedro, CA
www.portoflosangelas.org ; 310-732-3473
These original, beautifully restored railcars travel back and forth on a 1.5 mile track. There are 4 stations: Cruise Center, Downtown, Ports O'Call and Marina. At the Marina Station, vans offer lifts to 22nd Street and to the Cabrillo Aquarium. The cars run Friday through Monday. The fare is $1.00 per person for an all day pass.

Wayfarer's Chapel
5755 Palos Verdes Drive South, RPV, CA 90275
www.wayfarerschapel.org; 310-377-7919
Built in 1949 – 1951 by Lloyd Wright (Frank Lloyd Wright's son), the glass church is a national historical site. There is a garden area with a self guided walk outside and a visitor center with a gift shop inside.

White Point / Royal Palms County Beach
1000 Paseo Del Mar, San Pedro, CA
This property contains an upper and lower section. The upper area contains a park, baseball field, children's play area, restrooms, benches and historical plaques, plus a small parking lot. If you head down the paved street to the lower parking area ($6.00 fee), there are picnic tables, beach area and tide pools and more to explore.

Angel Gate Park

Chapter 10

Clubs & Organizations of the Peninsula

American Association of University Women
www.palosverdes.com/aauw/ ; 310-541-4630 Membership
P.O. Box 2443, Palos Verdes Peninsula, CA 90274

American Business Women's Association – Peninsula Chapter
310-544-2253
3200 La Rotonda Drive #212, Rancho Palos Verdes CA 90275

American Cetacean Society – L.A. Chapter
www.acs-la.org; 310-548-6279
P.O. Box 1391, San Pedro, CA 90733

Art At Your Fingertips
www.pvartcenter.org/community-detail.html#Fingertips ;
310-541-2479 – Palos Verdes Art Center

Assistance League of San Pedro-South Bay
www.assistanceleague.org ; 310-832-8355
1441 W. Eighth Street, San Pedro, CA 90732
(Auxiliaries: Assisteens, Colleagues, Las Primeras, Las
Profesionales, Spinnaker)

California Native Plant Society – South Coast Chapter
www.sccnps.org ; 310-831-0032
email: president@sccnps.org

Chamber Orchestra of the South Bay
www.palosverdes.com/chamberorchestra/; 310-373-3151
P.O. Box 2095, Palos Verdes Peninsula, CA 90274

Church Women United
310-377-2794
26847 W. Vale Road, Palos Verdes Estates, CA 90274

Coastwalk
www.coastwalk.org ; 1-800-550-6854
825 Gravenstein Hwy. North, Suite 8, Sebastopol, CA 95472

Community Assn. of the Peninsula
310-544-0403
27570 Crossfield Drive, Rolling Hills Estates, CA 90274

CORBA - PV
www.mtbpv.org ; sbmbc.com

Docent Council of the Palos Verdes Art Center
www.pvartcenter.org/docent.html ; 310-541-2479

Elks Club – San Pedro Lodge
310-831-0624
1748 Cumbre Drive, San Pedro, CA 90732

Empty Saddle Club
310-377-9059

Embroiders Guild of America – Azure Verde Chapter
www.geocities.com/AzureVerdeEGA/ ;
310-378-2577

Ernie Howlett Park Tennis Club
310-377-1577
4045 Palos Verdes Dr. N., Rolling Hills Estates, CA 90274

Friends of the Croatian Cultural Center
310-833-0103
510 W. 7th Street, San Pedro, CA

Friends of Madrona Marsh
www.friendsofmadronamarsh.com ;
P.O. Box 5078, Torrance, CA 90510

Friends of School Music for PVUSD
310-541-2025
P.O. Box 2721, Palos Verdes Peninsula, CA 90275

Great Books Discussion Group
310-545-5498

Happy Hats for Kids
310-326-8409
24 Dapplegray Lane, RHE, CA 90274

Harbor Interfaith Shelter
310-831-0603
664 W. 10th Street, San Pedro, CA 90731

Help The Homeless Help Themselves
310-544-7203
P.O. Box 3363, Palos Verdes Peninsula, CA 90274

Kiwanis Club of Rolling Hills Estates
310-378-5813
P.O. Box 2856, Palos Verdes Peninsula, CA 90274

Las Amigas de Las Lomas
310-548-3663
P.O. Box 2515, Palos Verdes Peninsula, CA 90274

League of Women Voters of Palos Verdes Peninsula/SP
www.palosverdes.com/lwv; 310-784-7787
P.O. Box 2933, Palos Verdes, CA 90274

Lions Club of Palos Verdes Peninsula
310-373-2568
2564 Via Carrillo, Palos Verdes Estates, CA 90274

Los Cancioneros Master Chorale
310-297-2613

Los Serenos de Pointe Vicente (Docents)
www.losserenos.org ; 310-544-5260

The Luminaries
310-544-9626
P.O. Box 3097, Rolling Hills Estates, CA 90274

Mary and Joseph League of Palos Verdes
310-377-4867 x. 256

National Charity League, Peninsula Chapter
310-5471602
353 West 6th Street, San Pedro, CA 90731

Navy League of the U.S., PVP Council
310-377-1607
P.O. Box 2116, Palos Verdes Peninsula, CA 90274

Neighborhood Alert on Drugs & Alcohol
310-373-7050
904 Silver Spur Road, Suite 208, Rolling Hills Estates, CA 90274

New Neighbors Of P.V. Peninsula
310-377-4112
P.O. Box 4181, Palos Verdes Estates, CA 90274
www.palosverdes.com/newneighbors

Palos Verdes Amateur Radio Club
www.palosverdes.com/pvarc/ or email: pvarc@msn.com
P.O. Box 2316, Palos Verdes Peninsula, CA 90274

Palos Verdes Art Center Artists
www.pvartcenter.org/organizations.html ; 310-541-2479
Includes the following organizations: Artists Open Group, Pacific
Arts Group, Paletteers, Palos Verdes Painters, Peninsula Artists,
Rembrandt Crew and Third Dimension

Palos Verdes / South Bay Audubon
P.O. Box 2582,   Palos Verdes, CA 90274
310-782-7527 (Wild Birds Unlimited)
or 310-539-0050; Imconsult.com/pvaudubon

Palos Verdes Ballet Association
310-377-6663
26A Peninsula Center, RHE, CA 90274

Palos Verdes Bridge Club
310-378-4803

Palos Verdes Bicycle Club
www.palosverdes.com/pvbikeclub ; 310-377-3516
email: pvbikeclub@palosverdes.com

Palos Verdes Estates Neighborhood Watch
310-373-1318
P.O. Box 925, Palos Verdes Estates, CA 90274

Palos Verdes Gem & Mineral Society
310-325-3139

Palos Verdes Junior Women's Club
310-377-7464
P.O. Box 1, Palos Verdes Estates, CA 90274

Palos Verdes Loop Trail Project
6 Limetree Lane Portuguese Bend, CA 90275

Palos Verdes Peninsula Association of Realtors
310-377-4873
627 Silver Spur Road, Suite 106, Rolling Hills Estates, CA 90274

Palos Verdes Peninsula Chamber of Commerce
310-377-8111
440 Palos Verdes Dr. N., Rolling Hills Estates, CA 90274

Palos Verdes Peninsula Coordinating Council
310-377-0735
P.O. Box 2304, Palos Verdes Peninsula, CA 90274

Palos Verdes Peninsula Democratic Club
310-377-0659
P.O. Box 2234, Palos Verdes Peninsula, CA 90274

Palos Verdes Peninsula Horsemens Association
www.pvpha.org ; 310-325-4903
P.O. Box 4153, Palos Verdes Peninsula, CA 90274

Palos Verdes Peninsula Land Conservancy
www.pvplc.org ; 310-541-7613
P.O. Box 3427, Palos Verdes Peninsula, CA 90274

Palos Verdes Pony Club
310-541-3452

Palos Verdes Symphonic Band
310-541-4520
P.O. Box 2041, Palos Verdes Peninsula, CA 90274

Peninsula Committee For The L.A. Philharmonic
310-377-3189
P.O. Box 2122, Palos Verdes Peninsula, CA 90274

Peninsula Council of PTA's
310-373-9966
3801 Via La Selva, Palos Verdes Estates, CA 90274

Peninsula Education Foundation
310-378-2278
P.O. Box 2632, Palos Verdes Peninsula, CA 90274

Peninsula Friends of the Library
310-541-2757
P.O. Box 2361, Palos Verdes Peninsula, CA 90274

Peninsula Seniors
310-377-3003; www.pvseniors.org
30928 Hawthorne Blvd., Ranch Palos Verdes, CA 90275

Peninsula Symphony Association
310-544-0320
P.O. Box 2602, Palos Verdes Peninsula, CA 90274

Portuguese Bend Pony Club
www.portuguesebend.ponyclub.org ; 310-544-6009

Portuguese Bend Riding Club
310-377-3507

Rancho Palos Verdes Neighborhood Watch
rpvnw@ix.netcom.com

Rancho Palos Verdes Senior's Bridge Group
310-541-8114 at Hesse Park

Rolling Hills Estates Pepper Tree Foundation
310-377-1577 at City Hall
4045 Palos Verdes Drive North, RHE, CA 90274

Rotary Club of Palos Verdes Peninsula
310-791-7476

Salvation Army of Rancho Palos Verdes
310-377-0481
30840 Hawthorne Boulevard, Rancho Palos Verdes, CA 90275

Sandpipers
310-374-1748
P.O. Box 72, Hermosa Beach, CA 90254

Sierra Club, P.V.-South Bay Group
www.angeles.sierraclub.org/pvsb; 310-378-1477
P.O. Box 2464, Palos Verdes Peninsula, CA 90274

South Bay Archery Club
www.southbayarchery.net ; 310-832-2282

South Coast Botanic Garden Foundation
www.southcoastbotanicgarden.org ; 310-544-1948
26300 Crenshaw Blvd. Palos Verdes Peninsula, CA 90274
(On this website you will find a list of many additional gardening and
specific species of plant clubs if interested.)

South Bay Chamber Music Society, Inc.
www.palosverdes.com/sbcms ; 310-379-7055
P.O. Box 2313, Palos Verdes Peninsula, CA 90275

South Bay Wheelmen
www.southbaywheelmen.org ; 310-379-3204
P.O. Box 3224, Redondo Beach, CA 90277

South Bay Wildlife Rehabilitation
www.sbwr.org ; 310-378-9921
26363 Silver Spur Road, Rancho Palos Verdes, CA 90275

Surfrider Foundation, South Bay Chapter
www.surfrider-southbay.org ; 310-535-3116
P.O. Box 3825, Manhattan Beach, CA 90266

Toastmasters on the Peninsula
310-541-6034

Wagonwheel Ranch Horseback Rides
Patshorsebackrides.com ; 310-567-3582

Walk On The Wild Side / Las Candalistas
310-541-7936
P.O. Box 3655, Palos Verdes Peninsula, CA 90275

Meyler Street Beach Access

Chapter 11

Churches & Synagogues

We were amazed to discover the number of places to worship on the Peninsula. There is also a wide variety of types of faith represented, all existing in harmony next to each other, showing the diversity of the people here. Many of these buildings have interesting architecture and offer wonderful histories to learn about in connection with the development of this area.

Ascension Lutheran Church
26231 Silver Spur Road, RPV, CA 90275
310-373-0454

Rock Solid Christian Assembly
867 W. 10th Street, San Pedro, CA 90731
310-832-2788

Bethany Christian Fellowship
792 W. 10th Street, San Pedro, CA 90731
310-831-1150

Centurion Christian Fellowship
524 S. Pacific Avenue, San Pedro, CA 90731
310-548-3045

Chabad of Palos Verdes
28041 S. Hawthorne, RPV, CA 90275
310-544-5544

Christ Lutheran Church
28850 Western Ave., RPV, CA 90275
310-831-0848

Church of Jesus Christ of Latter-Day Saints
5845 West Crestridge Road, RPV, CA 90275
310-544-3531

Church of Jesus Christ of Latter-Day Saints
1635 W. 9th Street, San Pedro, CA 90732
310-833-9494

Community Christian Church
1903 W Summerland Street, RPV, CA 90275
310-832-7304

Congregation Ner Tamid Of South Bay
5721 Crestridge Road, RPV, CA 90275
310-377-6986

First Baptist Church of Palos Verdes
28 Moccasin Lane, RHE, CA 90275
310-378-1253

First Baptist Church of San Pedro
555 West 7th Street, San Pedro, CA 90731
310-548-1333

First Church of Christ, Scientist
4010 PV Drive North, RHE, CA 90274
310-375-7914

First Presbyterian Church of San Pedro
731 S. Averill Avenue, San Pedro, CA 90732
310-832-7597

First United Methodist Church of San Pedro
580 West 6th Street, San Pedro, CA 90731
310-548-1001

Good Shepherd Lutheran Church
1350 West 25th Street, San Pedro, CA 90731
310-833-3336

Holy Trinity Catholic Church
1292 W. Santa Cruz Street, San Pedro, CA 90732
310-548-6535

Hope Chapel of San Pedro
461 West 9th Street, San Pedro, CA 90731
310-832-4673

Iglesia Sion Assembly of God
555 12th Street, San Pedro, CA 90731
310-833-0869

La Rambla Presbyterian Church
1491 W. O'Farrell Street, San Pedro, CA 90731
310-833-6844

Lunada Bay Vineyard Christian Fellowship
2161 Via Olivera, PVE, CA 90274
310-544-1958

Mary Star of the Sea
853 7th Street, San Pedro, CA 90731
310832-6287

Mount Olive Lutheran Church
5975 Armaga Springs Road, RPV, CA 90275
310-377-8541

Mount Sinai Missionary Baptist Church
225 S. Mesa Street, San Pedro, CA 90731
310-833-3223

Neighborhood Church – United Church of Christ
415 Paseo Del Mar, PVE, CA 90274
310-378-9353

New Life Christian Church
28340 Highridge Road, RHE, CA 90274
326-4900

Ocean View Baptist Church
1900 S. Western Avenue, San Pedro, CA 90731
310833-4413

Pacific Unitarian Church
5621 Montemalaga Drive, RPV, CA 90275
310-378-9449

Peninsula Church of the Nazarene
811 West 11th Street, San Pedro, CA 90731
310-832-4200

Peninsula Community Church
5640 West Crestridge Road, RPV, CA 90275
310-377-4661

Rock Solid Christian Assembly
867 W. 10th Street, San Pedro, CA 90731
310-832-2788

Rolling Hills Covenant Church
2222 Palos Verdes Drive North, RHE, CA 90274
310-519-9406

Rolling Hills Seventh-Day Adventist Church
28340 Highridge Road, RHE, CA 90274
310-541-1819

Rolling Hills United Methodist Church
26438 Crenshaw Blvd., RHE, CA 90274
310-377-6771

Saint Francis Episcopal Church
2220 Via Rosa, PVE, CA 90274
310-375-4617

Saint John Fisher Catholic Church
5448 Crest Road, RPV, CA 90275
310-377-5571

Saint Luke's Presbyterian Church
26825 Rolling Hills Road, RHE, CA 90274
310-377-2825

Saint Paul's Lutheran Church
31290 Palos Verdes Drive West, RPV, CA 90275
310-377-6806

Saint Peter's By The Sea Presbyterian Church
6410 Palos Verdes Drive South, RPV, CA 90275
310-377-6882

Saint Peter's Episcopal
1648 W. 9th Street, San Pedro, CA 90731
310-831-2361

South Bay Evangelical Church
5640 Crestridge Road, RPV, CA 90275
310-265-0240

Temple Beth El & Center
1435 W. Seventh Street, San Pedro, CA
310-833-2467

Temple Heights Southern Baptist Church
888 W. Hamilton Avenue, San Pedro, CA 90731
310-831-5446

Trinity Lutheran Church
1450 W. 7th Street, San Pedro, CA 90731
310-832-1189

Victory Chapel
235 N. Gaffey Street, San Pedro, CA 90731
310-831-3835

Warren Chapel Christian Methodist Episcopal
1039 W. Elberon Ave., San Pedro, CA 90732
310-831-3249

Wayfarer's Chapel
5755 Palos Verdes Drive South, RPV, CA 90275
310-377-1650

Miraleste Median Trail

Chapter 12

Places To Play

Finding a place to enjoy your favorite sport or hobby can sometimes be difficult. So, below we have put together a list of locations where, if you can find a free moment, you can go play.

Please note that some of the establishments listed below are private and only open to members. Contact them for more information.

Archery
South Bay Archery Club   310-832-2822

Basketball
Angel's Gate Recreation Center - Outdoor   310-548-7705
Bogdanovich Recreation Center – Both   310-548-7590
Ladera Linda Community Center - Outdoor   310-541-7073
Leland Recreation Center - Outdoor   310-548-7706
Peck Park Recreation Center - Both   310-548-7580

Beach Access Trails
(look under their trail name for further details)
Abalone Cove
Bluff Cove
Cabrillo Beach
Lunada Bay Beach
Malaga Cove or R.A.T. Beach
Meyler & Barbara Streets
North Paseo Del Mar
Point Vicente Fishing Access
Shoreline Park / RPV-San Pedro City Line
Trump National Golf Course
White Point County Beach

Boating

Cabrillo Marina   310-732-2252
Cabrillo Way Marina   310-514-4985
Holiday Harbor Marina   310-833-4468
San Pedro Marina   310-519-8177
Shelter Point Yacht Club   310-832-7507
Siesta Harbor Cruises   310-831-1906
Spirit Cruises   310-548-8080

Bocce Ball

Bogdanovich Rec Center   310-548-7590
Harbor Blvd. Parkway, Berth 94

Point Vicente Lighthouse

Chess
Croatian Cultural Center   310-435-4667
Harbor Boulevard Parkway - Outdoor

Diving
Diving Charters, Inc.	909-279-DIVE
Magician Dive Boat	818-499-7101
Psalty Adventures	310-714-0548
Second Stage Ocean Sports	714-539-5128
Westerly Charters	310-832-8304

Equestrian Activities
Chandler Park	310-377-1577
Dapplegray Park	310-377-0360
Empty Saddle Club	310-377-9059
Ernie Howlett Park	310-377-1577
Palos Verdes Stables	310-375-9005
Portuguese Bend Riding Club	310-377-3507
RH Equestrian Center	310-541-9487
Seahorse Riding Academy	310-541-5921
Wagonwheel Ranch Trail Rides	310-567-3582

Golfing
Los Verdes Country Club	310-377-7888
Palos Verdes Golf Club	310-375-2533
Rolling Hills Country Club	310-326-4343
Sea Air Golf Course	310-543-1583
Trump National Golf Course	310-265-5000

Hang Gliding
Wind Sports	310-474-3502
Xtreme Sky Adventures	310-374-5132

Paddle Tennis
Ladera Linda Community Center   310-541-7073

Sport Fishing
22nd Street Landing	310-832-8304
Los Angeles Harbor Sport Fishing	310-547-9916

Swimming
Bally Total Fitness	310-732-2100
Equinox	310-697-1016
Jack Kramer Club	310-326-4921
L.A. County Junior Lifeguard Program	310-939-7214
Palos Verdes Beach & Athletic Club	310-375-8777
Peck Pool	310-548-2434
Peninsula Bay Cities Swim School	310-541-3664
Rolling Hills Estates Swim Program	310-377-1577
Spectrum Club	310-541-2582
YMCA – San Pedro & Peninsula	310-832-4211

196

Tennis

Daniels Field Sports Center	310-548-7728
Ernie Howlett Park Courts	310-541-4585
Jack Kramer Club	310-326-4404
Palos Verdes Tennis Club	310-373-6326
Peck Park Courts	310-541-2582
Peninsula Racquet Club	310-541-2523
Rolling Hills Estates Tennis Club	310-541-4585
South Bay Tennis Club	310-530-8212
Upper Point Vicente Court	

Windsurfing / Kiteboarding

Captain Kirk's	310-833-3397

Aerial view of Peninsula

Malaga Cove School

Chapter 13

History of the Peninsula

The history of the Peninsula started when this area first rose out of the sea in the form of a lush, tropical island, sometime between 60 and 23 million years ago. The exact date is uncertain as this hill sank and rose from the sea a total of three different times. Most recently it rose around 30,000 years ago. Sediment then formed between this island and the mountains north and east of us, creating the Los Angeles basin and connecting us to the mainland.

The first known people to live here existed between 14,000 and 11,000 years ago. They shared the land with mastadons, mammoths, giant bison, saber toothed tigers, dire wolves and others. Archeologists believe the "Los Angeles Man", uncovered next to Ballona Creek in Playa del Rey, and the 13,000 year old "Arlington Springs Woman", found on Santa Rosa Island, are from that time.

Towards the end of the last Ice Age about 11,000 years ago, our local climate started shifting from a tropical environment to a much more arid one. About 4,000 years ago, this drying phase peaked and many of the plants and animals that lived here became extinct. The "La Brea Woman" found in the La Brea Tar Pits walked the land during this time.

Mankind invented new ways to live and find food. Fewer people lived inland, relying on deer, antelope, rabbits and seeds, as the environment became more desert like. Along the Coast, shellfish, marine mammals and sea life become much more important. Riparian Habitat, like that found beside streams and rivers, became essential to man as it attracted different types of plants, animals and migratory birds. The Los Angeles River and White Point, with its natural springs, became gathering spots. The population of the Palos Verdes Peninsula and the South Bay at this time was 200 – 300.

Starting about 4,000 years ago the climate started returning to a wetter environment and inland man invented the spear thrower. About this time, Shoshonean Indians began arriving from the East. Through their dominance, they eventually become the primary people. Population grew about 10 fold with some groups possibly reaching 300 members.

The first Spanish explorer to see this coast was Juan Rodriguez Cabrillo in 1542. He passed through San Pedro Bay and named it the bay of smokes, probably due to Indian fires, before landing briefly on Catalina Island. The next Spanish explorer to come here was Sebastian Vizcaino, 60 years later. He landed, and explored on foot, visiting what is today Harbor Park. For the next 109 years, the only contact between the Spanish and the Shoshonean Indians was the occasional Manila gallion stopping for food and water.

In 1769, the first California mission was established in San Diego. Over the next decade, the San Gabriel and Los Angeles Missions were also established.

In 1784, Rancho San Pedro was deeded to Juan Jose Dominguez, one of the soldiers who accompanied Padre Serra. The deed was a reward from the King for a lifetime of service to the Spanish Army. It included all of the Peninsula and part of the South Bay.

The Indians, called Gabrielinos by the Spanish, were rounded up and brought to the missions for religious conversion and control. Livestock was brought in and the Indians were forced into labor. In 1810, a 17 year old Jose Sepulveda was given permission to raise livestock on and around the Palos Verdes area. He based his operation, and made his home, near Harbor Lake, as the Indians had done before him. After a three decade long legal battle, Sepulveda won the Peninsula land in a court decision, although further legal wrangling over ownership of the Hill would not be complete until 1882.

The Peninsula changed owners over the next decades. In 1821, Mexico gained independence from Spain and the Peninsula changed from Spanish rule to Mexican. Then, in 1846-7 the United States Army took control from Mexico and the Peninsula became part of U.S. territory. Finally, in 1882, most of the Peninsula was sold to Jotham Bixby. The population increased during this time from 75 in 1836 to 911 by 1880.

Whaling, which had started in the early 1800's, was ending as the whale population was being decimated at sea, and on land most trees and bushes had been cut down to fuel the fires necessary in rendering blubber into oil. The Portuguese Bend whaling station was abandoned and pressure was transferred to other marine life, such as otters and seals. Finally, in 1913, all fur seals and otters became protected in California and Alaska, narrowly saving them from extinction.

In the years around 1890, about 2,000 Japanese immigrated to the area and became successful at fishing and farming. In 1913, the population of people in San Pedro was 8,100 and Frank A Vanderlip bought most of the Peninsula (16,000 acres) and planned the development of the entire property. Malaga Cove was designed and finished according to his vision. Much of the early infrastructure and the planting of over 100,000 trees across the Peninsula were due to him. In 1917, Tamisi Tagami started building the White Point resort hotel and spa and soon after Ramon Sepulveda developed

Royal Palms Family Club on the beach to the right. The outdoor fire places and dance floors survive today. A tsunami destroyed the spa's swimming pool in 1926 and the Long Beach earthquake of 1933 cut off the flow to the mineral springs at White Point Spa. This combined with the Great Depression caused the hotel to close forever. Unfortunately, the Great Depression and then the war put an end to Vanderlip's plans as well. Next on his itinerary was to turn today's Bluff Cove into a grand yacht harbor. Lunada Bay was also to have a breakwall built for safe swimming and a grand beach club.

In 1926, Point Vicente Lighthouse was built and soon after the developers of Rolling Hills and Palos Verdes Estates started formalizing the bridle trail system across the hill. 14" guns were installed at White Point and when they were test fired in 1927, windows shattered across San Pedro. In 1935, the Palos Verdes Corporation planted all the Pepper trees on both sides of Palos Verdes Drive North.

With the United States' entrance into World War II, the situation for Japanese immigrants changed dramatically. In 1942, all Japanese on the Peninsula were forcibly entered into internment camps. Most lost all of their property and possessions.

During the 40's, houses began replacing farms more and more. Into the 50's, lots could be purchased on the Hill for $1,000. Since that time, prices have continued to rise as more people have realized the beauty of this area and the value of its rural charm.

Today, just as in the past, the beauty and value of this area continues to rise in many ways. Active citizens, local city politicians and volunteer organizations are all contributing their efforts to improving life in our community.

Postscript

We hope that you use and enjoy this book. We have tried to walk a fine line between sharing what we know and disclosing too much of what are for many, their personal favorite spots. Not all trails we know of are in this book. Some were left out because we felt they encroached too closely on private property; some because of their seasonal nature; and many because we do not like to promote bushwhacking through canyons and other areas that see only very limited traffic.

We have tried our best to provide correct and up-to-date information in regards to facilities, organizations, maps and trail descriptions. However, information does change and we apologize for any misinformation.

If you would like to share your comments and feelings, you may email us at pvpoutdoorguide@earthlink.net or check out our website at home.earthlink.net/~pvpoutdoorguide .

Bridle Trail tunnel

Bibliography

Randall, Laura. *60 Hikes Within 60 Miles – Los Angeles.* Menasha Ridge Press, Birmingham, AL, 2006.

Ackerman, Pat. *Palos Verde Peninsula Place Names: What is it? How did it get its name?* 1991.

Adventure Magazine, April Edition, 2006

Bauman, Jack. Prepared by Roderman, Mary. *Peninsula Pastimes: Recollections of an Oldtimer.* Rancho de los Palos Verdes Historical Society & Museum, 1995.

Bauman, Gus. *History of Palos Verdes Estates, California.* Angel Press, Monterey, CA, 1975.

Bean, Lowell John and Thomas C. Blackburn. *Native Californians: A Theoretical Retrospective.* Ballena Press, 1976.

Brundige, Don & Sharron. *Mountain Biking L.A. County: Southern Section.* B-D Enterprises, 1996.

Brundige, Don & Sharron. *Bicycle Rides L.A. County.* B-D Enterprises, 1989.

City of Palos Verdes Estates – Office of the City Clark. *Palos Verdes Estates Resident Handbook.* March, 2006.

Department of Planning Building and Code Enforcement: Rancho Palos Verdes. *Conceptual Trails Plan.* 1993.

205

Dye, Barbara. *A Driving Tour of the Palos Verdes Peninsula.* Blickidy Press, 1992.

Dye, Barbara and Mary Ellen Richardson. *Best Hikes On The Palos Verdes Peninsula: A Palos Verdes Peninsula Land Conservancy Guide.* Bookmasters, Inc, Ashland, OH, 2007.

Fink, Augusta. *Palos Verdes Peninsula: Time and the Terraced Land.* Western Tanager Press, Santa Cruz, 1987.

Forrest, Michael R. *Palos Verdes Field Trip Guide.* Southern California Earthquake Center, USC, 1994.

Gales, Donald Moore. *Handbook of Wildflowers, Weeds, Wildlife and Weather of Palos Verdes Peninsula.* Folda Roll Company, 2003.

Hanson, A.E., *Rolling Hills: The Early Years.* City of Rolling Hills, Typecraft, Inc., Pasadena, CA.

Hawley, Michael. *The Fowler Trail.* Pamphlet. Eagle Scout Troop 234.

Heizer, Robert F., and Albert F. Elsasser, *The Natural World of the California Indians.* University of California Press, Berkley, CA, 1983.

Jankowiak, William R. *Historical Perspective, Rancho San Pedro to Lot 49 – Section 7: Ownership and Land Use.* 1997.

Marinella, Carmen. *The Palos Verdes Peninsula: A History.* 1993.

Marinella, Carmen & Dye, Barbara. *Palos Verdes: A Place Set Apart.* Video Recording

McKinney, John. *Walking Southern California: A Day Hikers Guide.* Harper-Collins West, 1994.

McKinney, John. *Walking the California Coast: One Hundred Adventures Along the West Coast.* Harper-Collins West, 1994.

McKinney, John. *Walking Southern California: A Day Hikers Guide.* Olympus Press, 1987.

Morgan, Delane. *The Palos Verdes Story.* Review Publications, Palos Verdes Peninsula, CA, 1982.

Palos Verdes Peninsula Horsemens Association. *PVPHA Trail Guide.* Fourth Edition September 2004.

Palos Verdes Peninsula Land Conservancy. *Open Spaces Newsletter.* Quarterly Issues, 1994 – Present.

Schad, Jerry & Krupp, Don. *50 Southern California Bicycle Trips.* Touchstone Press, Beaverton, OR, 1976.

Schad, Jerry. *Afoot and Afield in Los Angeles County.* Wilderness Press, 1991.

Swaffield, Roland G., *Saga of the City of Rolling Hills.* Crawford Press, Long Beach, CA, 1958.

Internet Web Sites:

ranchopalosverdes.areaconnect.com/churches.htm
www.ci.rolling-hills-estates.ca.us/
www.earth.google.com
www.friendsofmadronamarsh.com
www.mtbpv.org
www.neighborhoodchurchpve.org
www.pvplc.org
www.palosverdes.com
www.palosverdeschamber.com
www.palosverdes.com/rpv/
www.pvld.org
www.sanpedrochamber.com
www.sanpedro.com
www.terranea.com
www.trumpgolf.com/trumplosangeles/index.asp
www.wayfarerschapel.com

Television:

Science Channel. *Islands of the Pygmy Mammoths.* May 22, 2006,
8:00 pm Episode.

INDEX